Praise for *Church Planting by the Book*

"Elbert Smith is a seasoned trainer of church planters. In *Church Planting by the Book*, he traces the New Testament story line in order to provide biblical guidelines and insights for church planting. Recommended for church planters, potential church planters, pastors and students."

—Bruce Ashford, PhD
Provost and Dean of the Faculty, Southeastern Baptist Theological Seminary
Editor, *Theology and Practice of Mission: God the Church and the Nations*

"In his book, *Church Planting by the Book*, Elbert Smith gleans out of the Acts narrative a number of timeless guiding principles and examples to guide the church planter in the twenty-first century. It is refreshing to have a book on church planting that unequivocally acknowledges the primary role of the Holy Spirit in church planting."

—R. Bruce Carlton, DTh
WMU Professor of Missions, Oklahoma Baptist University
Global Church Planting Consultant

"In his book, *Church Planting by the Book*, Elbert explores the common threads of the work of God in and through the early church in order to understand better the ways of God for church planting today. So grab yourself a cup of coffee, as I'm sure Elbert has his, and allow him to walk you through the nine church plants in the book of Acts!"

—John Charping, PhD
Mid-America Baptist Theological Seminary
Associate Cluster Leader in East Indonesia and Beyond
International Mission Board, SBC

"Given our tremendous task to take the gospel to the world, [Elbert Smith] deeply desires that we build our work on the Word. You cannot read this book without longing to see God work in a mighty way around the world."

—Chuck Lawless, PhD
Vice President for Graduate Studies and Ministry Centers,
Southeastern Baptist Theological Seminary
Global Theological Education Consultant, International Mission Board, SBC

Church Planting by the Book

E. Elbert Smith

PUBLICATIONS
Fort Washington, PA 19034

Church Planting by the Book
Published by CLC Publications

U.S.A.
P.O. Box 1449, Fort Washington, PA 19034
UNITED KINGDOM
CLC International (UK)
Unit 5, Glendale Avenue, Sandycroft, Flintshire, CH5 2QP

ISBN (paperback): 978-1-61958-192-0
ISBN (e-book): 978-1-61958-193-7

Unless otherwise noted, Scripture quotations are from the New American Standard Bible®, copyright © 1960, 1962, 1963, 1968, 1971, 1972, 1973, 1975, 1977, 1995 by The Lockman Foundation. Used by permission.

Scripture quotations marked ESV are from the Holy Bible, English Standard Version®, copyright © 2001 by Crossway, a publishing ministry of Good News Publishers. Used by permission. All rights reserved.

Scripture quotations marked NIV are from the Holy Bible, New International Version®, NIV®, © 1973, 1978, 1984, 2011 by Biblica, Inc.®. Used by permission. All rights reserved worldwide.

Scripture quotations marked HCSB are from the Holman Christian Standard Bible®, Copyright © 1999, 2000, 2002, 2003, 2009 by Holman Bible Publishers. Used by permission. Holman Christian Standard Bible®, Holman CSB®, and HCSB® are federally registered trademarks of Holman Bible Publishers.

Italics in Scripture quotations are the emphasis of the author.

Contents

Foreword

"There is nothing new under the sun," wrote the preacher (Eccles. 1:9). But a fresh recovery of seasoned, Bible-centered principles can often give rise to new waves of effectiveness. Nowhere is this more visible than in the current missiological arena.

While in recent centuries missionaries have most often been considered merely evangelists on foreign soil, we are now witnessing a new generation bent on recovering first-century practices. There is a growing realization that a "threefold cord" is both scriptural and genuinely effective. "Sent ones" are learning to practice evangelism and discipleship with the objective of planting reproducing churches.

This recovery of first-century focus shapes the organization I am privileged to serve. While utilizing the many gifts entrusted by the Spirit to the church, our personnel are gripped with the simple truth that in addition to evangelizing and making disciples, we must also focus on planting healthy, reproducing New Testament churches in the most remote corners of this globe. Church planting has become a barometer by which we measure engagement among the world's people groups.

This brings me to the book you now hold in your hands, *Church Planting by the Book*. If I could have only one book on church planting (other than the Scripture, of course) this

would be the book I would choose. Elbert Smith has challenged those of us engaged in God's church-planting mission
with a study that is both remarkable in its insight and intrigu-
ing in its simplicity. Even as you read this book, you will find
yourself wanting to immediately put the principles into practice and pass them on to others.

The practical nature of this book should not surprise you.
Elbert Smith is no mere theorist. After first serving over a
decade on the field, he was then called upon to direct a major
missionary training school in North America. During the en-
suing years, Smith has trained literally thousands of mission
personnel who are currently serving around the world. These
missionaries are employing the practical and clearly enunci-
ated teachings you now have the benefit of reviewing for yourself.

Elbert Smith will be the first to tell you that there is nothing original about what he has written. After all, it has all been
recorded in the book of Acts and proven effective through
the centuries. But Smith's distillation of these truths, coupled
with practical, doable application creates a growing conviction
of the necessity of practicing them today. After all, the Great
Commission has yet to be fulfilled—and a lost world awaits
the gospel.

Tom Elliff
Past President, International Mission Board
Southern Baptist Convention

Introduction

What an exciting but challenging time. You and your family are planning to leave the familiar surroundings of home for a new country to take the good news to those who have not heard it. Or your church has embraced a people group[1] that has not heard of the Savior, desiring that those within that ethnic group will hear the good news and that an indigenous, multiplying church will be planted in their midst. Or you have seen the biblical truth of God's love for the nations,[2] and you desire to dig deeper into what His Word says about church planting among them.

God's Word, used by the Holy Spirit, is your primary source of guidance in all of life, but where do you go to understand what the Bible says about the missionary[3] task? Where in Scripture would you look to find specific insight regarding church planting, whether across town or across the globe?

Certainly God can give insight to the church planter from any part of Scripture. For example, I remember personal insights that I gained from Ecclesiastes prior to my wife and I returning to Mexico for our second term as church planters. After our first term, Kay and I had pastored thirteen years in the United States (including at a church plant in Fort Wayne, Indiana), and we were about to return to Mexico. As I read through the Old Testament in my quiet time, I came to Ecclesiastes 11:2: "Divide your portion to seven, or even to eight, for you do not know what misfortune may occur on the earth." I sensed in my spirit that it would be wise to apply that verse to our work that term, and I made sure after we arrived in Mexico that my wife, Kay, and I worked with several groups at the same time in our church-planting efforts. One of those groups became a solid church that has since started other churches. Some of the groups, however, faced "misfortune," and no church was planted from them. I feel that the Holy Spirit guided me through the Ecclesiastes passage—even though church planting is not the primary topic of Ecclesiastes. God can give insight from the Old Testament or from the Gospels, despite the fact that church planting is not the primary topic of any book in those portions of Scripture.

Nine Churches

In order for us to lay a foundation for how to plant the first church in a churchless city, we must turn to the New Testament, and primarily to the book of Acts. In both Acts and in Paul's epistles, we find nine groups of new believers, in nine different cities, described by the word *church*. In the book of Acts we also encounter descriptions for each of these nine churches. In this book, we will examine these nine New Testament churches. The Holy Spirit who inspired Luke to write these passages in the days of the early church gives insight and application for the listening church planter today.

It is impossible to say how many churches were planted between the ascension of our Lord Jesus in Acts 1 and Paul's arrival in Rome in Acts 28. Besides the nine that are definitively described in the book of Acts, the New Testament mentions other cities where many other churches may have been started. When Paul writes to the Galatian churches, for instance, he speaks of "the *churches of Judea* which were in Christ" (Gal. 1:22), referring to a time perhaps little more than four or five years after Christ's ascension. First Thessalonians 2:14 also mentions "the churches of God in Christ Jesus that are in Judea." We know of only one church in Judea from the book of Acts: the church in Jerusalem. Obviously, as we see from these verses, there were others.

Following Philip's ministry in Samaria, we are told only of baptized believers (see Acts 8:12) and of Peter and John "preaching the gospel to many villages of the Samaritans" (8:25). No churches are mentioned in Acts 8, but the next chapter tells us of "the church throughout all Judea and Galilee *and Samaria*" (9:31), which describes the time following Paul's first post-conversion visit to Jerusalem. Quite possibly many churches existed in Galilee and Samaria shortly after this visit.[4] After the amazing conversion of Cornelius' household in Acts 10, we assume that a church was planted in Caesarea as well, although neither the book of Acts nor the rest of the New Testament clearly says so.[5]

As we've noted, however, the book of Acts contains nine descriptions of churches being planted, and we find each one of them called a church either in Acts or in Paul's epistles:

- Jerusalem (see 5:11; 8:1)
- Antioch (see 11:26; 13:1)

From Paul's first missionary journey (to the province of Galatia):

- Pisidian Antioch (see Acts 14:21–23; Gal. 1:2)
- Iconium (see Acts 14:21–23; Gal. 1:2)
- Lystra (see Acts 14:21–23; Gal. 1:2)

From Paul's second journey (to the region of Macedonia):
- Philippi (see Phil. 4:15; 2 Cor. 8:1)
- Thessalonica (see 1 Thess. 1:1; 2 Thess. 1:1)
- Corinth (see 1 Cor. 1:2)

And from Paul's third journey (to Asia):
- Ephesus (see Acts 20:17)

Common Threads and Unique Insights

As we examine these nine definite church plants, we will look for *common threads* and *unique insights* in the book of Acts and in other passages that can provide guidance for church planters today. Common threads refers to those principles and patterns that we see repeated in many of the church plants in the book of Acts which church planters today can emulate. In addition, we can gain unique insights from particular occurrences that took place in various church plants in Acts. Both can inform the church planter today.

Common Threads

One common thread that we find in Acts regarding church planting includes the five elements of a healthy church first seen in the Jerusalem church in Acts 2. These characteristics of a healthy church are found throughout the book of Acts in the descriptions of all nine churches.

Other common threads regarding church planting that we see again and again in the new churches of Acts (and which constitute Paul's church-planting pattern) include the following elements:
- Praying
- Beginning with a plan or custom

- Starting a church where God's Word has already been sown
- Presenting the gospel on the authority of Scripture
- Depending upon the Holy Spirit to save and fill new believers
- Discipling those who believe
- Experiencing opposition
- Equipping leaders from within the new congregations
- Departing from a church plant and returning later to check on the new believers
- Multiplying disciples and churches

Unique Insights

We will also gain understanding from unique insights in the book of Acts regarding the following topics:

- Different ways in which the Holy Spirit guides church planters
- The challenges of church planters who do not understand the heart language of a people group
- Different locations in which church groups can meet
- The need to work as a tentmaker (to perform secular work to provide one's support) at times

The Holy Spirit who guided Luke to write the book of Acts applies these common threads and unique insights to church planters who today follow His direction.

Scriptural Commands and Applications

At times in the book of Acts, we see clear scriptural commands given to all believers. We must carefully follow these commands in all church plants in every age. The doctrine that was "once for all delivered to the saints" (Jude 3, ESV) is the critical foundation for every new church.

However, much of the book of Acts consists of narrative passages that contain neither doctrinal teaching nor clear scriptural commands given to all believers. The Holy Spirit uses these narrative passages to guide those of us who are church planters, as he did for me with the passage from Ecclesiastes, showing us how to apply insights from these passages in specific ways that are best for each situation.

Let's get started with our examination of church planting in the Word of God: church planting by the Book. May these insights from Acts, like a little water that primes the pump to provide a long supply of water, turn our attention to the book of Acts as the primary scriptural source for guidance in planting the first church in any city.

1

THE CHURCH IN JERUSALEM, PART 1

Acts 1:9–2:41

The Jerusalem church was born in the wake of a prayer meeting. When Jesus returned to heaven following His earthly ministry and His resurrection from the dead, He left behind 120 believers—the eleven apostles, His mother Mary and His brothers, and others—who gathered together to wait for the Holy Spirit, whom Jesus had promised to send, and to pray. As they sought the Lord together, God sent the Holy Spirit in power, and many in Jerusalem saw and believed the message of the gospel. Thus began the era of church planting.

The book of Acts dedicates a great deal of attention to the church at Jerusalem in chapters 1–7, portions of 9 and 11 and all of 12. Because of this, we will devote two chapters of this book to this first and highly visible church. In chapter 1 we will discuss how the Jerusalem church began. Chapter 2 will then look at the description of this church, which is the model for a healthy church, and examine the church's growth and expansion.

The account of the founding of the Jerusalem church emphasizes the prayer on the part of the 120 and their being filled with the Holy Spirit on the day of Pentecost. Many Jews were

gathered in Jerusalem at that time for the Feast of Pentecost—
men and women from countries all over the known world. As
the 120 were filled with the Holy Spirit, they began to speak
the gospel in many different languages, and they sowed seed
broadly in the heart languages of their hearers. This powerful
testimony was followed by a clear presentation of the gospel by
Peter. The Holy Spirit's conviction that day drew three thousand individuals to repent, believe and be baptized.

Each of these details provides insights into the church-
planting task today. Let's look at them, one by one.

Prayer

> After [Jesus] had said these things, He was lifted up while
> [the disciples] were looking on, and a cloud received Him out
> of their sight. And as they were gazing intently into the sky
> while He was going, behold, two men in white clothing stood
> beside them. They also said, "Men of Galilee, why do you
> stand looking into the sky? This Jesus, who has been taken up
> from you into heaven, will come in just the same way as you
> have watched Him go into heaven."
>
> Then they returned to Jerusalem from the mount called
> Olivet, which is near Jerusalem, a Sabbath day's journey away.
> When they had entered the city, they went up to the upper
> room where they were staying; that is, Peter and John and
> James and Andrew, Philip and Thomas, Bartholomew and
> Matthew, James the son of Alphaeus, and Simon the Zealot,
> and Judas the son of James. These all with one mind were
> continually devoting themselves to prayer, along with the
> women, and Mary the mother of Jesus, and with His broth-
> ers. (Acts 1:9–14)

As is often the case in Scripture, the first reference to a
topic is filled with important insight. This first description

of a church plant begins with an emphasis on prayer—a very important insight for church-planting teams today. As soon as Acts 1 moves from the ascension of the Lord Jesus to the subsequent actions of the apostles, it describes them as being in prayer: "These all with one mind were continually devoting themselves to prayer." The team that God had put in place for the planting of the Jerusalem church began with a focus on unified prayer.

Begin with prayer, and make it foundational in all you do.

This emphasis on prayer is found throughout the description of the Jerusalem church. In Acts 2:1 we see the 120 gathered together on the day of Pentecost, brought together apparently *by prayer*. The healing miracle that Peter and John perform and their subsequent arrest in Acts 3 and 4 unfold as the two disciples are going up to the temple *to pray*. The early church leaders did not just talk about prayer; they were actively engaged in it. In Acts 6 we read that seven Spirit-filled men were named to serve tables[1] so that the twelve apostles could devote themselves *to prayer* and the ministry of the Word. Following the martyrdom of Stephen in Acts 7, Luke's story moves largely to locations outside Jerusalem, but when the narrative returns to Jerusalem in chapter 12 and Peter is arrested, we read that "prayer for him was being made fervently by the church to God" (12:5).

The Jerusalem church was birthed in prayer. It was led by people who prayed and was characterized by prayer. The first application from Jerusalem for the church-planting

team today is this: begin with prayer, and make it foundational in all you do!

Responding to a God-Controlled Event

> When the day of Pentecost had come, they were all together
> in one place. And suddenly there came from heaven a noise
> like a violent rushing wind, and it filled the whole house
> where they were sitting. And there appeared to them tongues
> as of fire distributing themselves, and they rested on each one
> of them. (Acts 2:1–3)

The second chapter of Acts begins with an amazing God-
controlled event: the descending of the Holy Spirit on the day
of Pentecost.

When life-changing acts of God happen,
be ready to respond with evangelism and church planting.

Fourteen hundred years before this occasion, Moses had
written about the three feasts that brought the nation together each year: the Feast of Unleavened Bread, the Feast of
the Harvest (or Weeks) and the Feast of the Ingathering (see
Exod. 23:15–17). The first, the Feast of Unleavened Bread, or
the Passover, had been filled with meaning for the 120 as they
witnessed Jesus Christ's death on the cross (see Luke 22:1–2).[2]
Now fifty days had passed, and it was time for the Feast of the
Harvest.[3] As the 120 were together in one place on that feast
day, a noise like a great wind filled the house, and what looked
like tongues of fire descended on each person in the room. At
this instant the believers were all filled with the Holy Spirit,

and many saw it and were drawn to salvation in Christ. The Jerusalem church was birthed!

This was an incredible, God-controlled event. No person could have caused it or planned it. Only God could have! The believers went out into the streets and began sharing the gospel with those who were open and interested as a result of the God-event.

Pentecost was a historical event that happened just as it did only once in history. God-controlled events, however, still take place in the world today and lead people to be open to the gospel and interested in Christ in a way that they were not before. No person could control a hurricane hitting Honduras or a tsunami rolling over Southeast Asia, but both were God-controlled events that provided opportunities for believers to share with people in ways that had not been possible before. The One who turned Satan's worst onslaught (Jesus' death on the cross) into salvation for all who believe can turn catastrophic events in the world into open doors for the gospel. In this narrative account in Acts 2 we see a second application[4] for the church-planting team today: when life-changing acts of God happen, we must be ready to respond with evangelism and church planting.

While Jesus' example compels us to care for people in a crisis and respond by meeting their needs (see Matt. 9:35–36), we know that the deepest need of all people is to be made right with their Creator. That deepest need is met only by the gospel. While believers should respond to catastrophic events by meeting needs, we can also be intentional about including evangelism and church planting in our response. A New Testament church would provide a lasting witness to God's love in a community affected by catastrophic events. When

Paul commands the Ephesian church, "Be careful how you walk, not as unwise men but as wise, making the most of your time" (Eph. 5:15–16), he uses a word for "time" that does not refer to ticks of a watch (the Greek language had a different word for that).[5] The word the Holy Spirit guided Paul to use for "time" could be translated "strategic opportunities." God-controlled events may produce strategic opportunities for evangelism and church planting, and we are to make the most of them. The church plant described in Acts 2 provides an example of how we can respond to such events today.

The Holy Spirit's Filling

> They were all filled with the Holy Spirit and began to speak with other tongues, as the Spirit was giving them utterance. (Acts 2:4)

The wind that filled the house and the "tongues as of fire" that "rested on each one of them" (2:3) are reminiscent of the glory of the Lord that filled the tabernacle in the wilderness as the cloud by day and the fire by night (see Exod. 40:34–38). That same glory of the Lord filled Solomon's temple after his prayer of dedication (see 2 Chron. 7:1–3) and then departed from that temple in Ezekiel's vision (see Ezek. 10:4, 18–19; 11:23). Paul refers to this glory of the Lord[6] as the Spirit who transforms believers (see 2 Cor. 3:18).

When the wind and the "tongues as of fire" appeared, the believers "were all filled with the Holy Spirit" (Acts 2:4), and they began to share the gospel boldly (see 2:11). Before His ascension, Jesus had commanded the apostles not to leave Jerusalem until they had received "what the Father had promised" (1:4).[7] He had specifically promised them that they would "receive power when the Holy Spirit" (1:8) came upon them, empowering them to be witnesses in Jerusalem and to the ends of the earth. The Holy Spirit filled the believers on the day of Pentecost, empowering them to share the gospel boldly, and then worked through them to plant the church in Jerusalem.

The work of the Holy Spirit is described repeatedly throughout the book of Acts. "Those who had believed" and repented at Peter's message on the day of Pentecost were promised that they would each receive the Holy Spirit (see Acts 2:44, 38). In Acts 4:8, Peter is filled with the Spirit as he responds to interrogation. In Acts 4:31, we are specifically told that the believers "were all filled with the Holy Spirit and began to speak the Word of God with boldness." From these and many other passages, we see that the normal sign or result of being filled with the Spirit in the book of Acts is to speak the Word of God with boldness.

The normal sign of being filled with the Spirit is speaking the Word of God with boldness.

In Acts 6:3, we read that one of the requirements of leadership was that a man be filled with the Spirit. It was the Spirit's infilling that empowered Stephen to boldly face martyrdom (see 7:55). The Samaritans who believed the gospel received the Holy Spirit (see 8:17). The converted persecutor named Saul was filled with the Holy Spirit (see 9:17). In Acts 10:19, the Holy Spirit guides Peter to go to Cornelius' house, and in verse 44 those in the house who believe receive the Holy Spirit.[8] Barnabas is described as "full of the Holy Spirit and of faith" (Acts 11:24) as he helps plant the church in Antioch.

Paul's first missionary journey began at the prompting of the Holy Spirit (see 13:2) and, in Acts 13:9, Paul is filled with the Spirit as he preaches in the first city of the first journey. The new believers in Galatia were "continually filled with joy and with the Holy Spirit" (13:52). The Holy Spirit guided the first church council (see 15:28), and He guided Paul, Silas and Timothy on Paul's second missionary journey (see 16:6–7). At the beginning of his third missionary journey, Paul determined whether or not twelve men were truly saved by asking them if they had received the Spirit, and after they believed in Jesus, they did receive the Spirit (see 19:2, 6). At the end of his third missionary journey, Paul was again guided by the Spirit and warned of challenging situations to come (see 19:21; 20:22–23).

Throughout all the missionary work in Acts, the role of the Holy Spirit is emphasized: He empowers, gives boldness and guides the church planter, and He fills every new believer.

From the very beginning of the Jerusalem church, throughout all the missionary work in Acts, the role of the Holy Spirit is emphasized: empowering, giving boldness to and guiding the church planters, and filling every new believer. The apostles were told by Jesus not to leave home without the Spirit's power; the church planter today can be greatly encouraged that he or she is not alone! God the Holy Spirit lives within believers, and He is all-powerful and all-wise! The church planter today must be careful to be filled with the Spirit, to walk in the Spirit daily, to be led by the Spirit (see Eph. 5:18; Gal. 5:16, 18).

Sharing in People's Heart Language

> Now there were Jews living in Jerusalem, devout men from every nation under heaven. And when this sound occurred, the crowd came together, and were bewildered because each one of them was hearing them speak in his own language. They were amazed and astonished, saying, "Why, are not all these who are speaking Galileans? And how is it that we each hear them in our own language to which we were born?" (Acts 2:5–8)

The second paragraph of Acts 2 describes all the believers sharing the wonders of God in the heart languages of the many who had gathered. What is described as speaking in other tongues in verse 4 is clarified in verses 6 and 8. Those listening each heard the message in their "own language," or dialect.[9] This is further clarified as the language "to which [they] were born." This would refer to one's mother tongue or heart language. The languages in which the believers spoke were the mother tongues of the hearers.

---

*On the day the Jerusalem church was born,
the good news was shared in the hearers' heart languages.*

While no command is given here that the gospel should be shared only in the heart language of the hearer, nor does this passage say that it is wrong to use a translator, we can certainly gain insight from this scripture that the gospel is best shared in the heart language or mother tongue of the hearer. Something seems wrong with announcing to people that we have a message from the Maker of heaven and earth who is their Creator, while we, His messengers, are not communicating that message in the people's language.

It will be helpful for those being sent out to plant churches to remember that they are not going to share a message from a foreign culture with people; rather, they are going to share a message with these people from the people's Creator. That message always comes across as less foreign and easier to understand when people hear it in their heart language. Surely sharing through a translator or in a trade language is infinitely better than not sharing at all; however, on the day the Jerusalem church was born, the good news was shared in the hearers' heart languages.

Broad Seed Sowing to Prepare Hearts for the Gospel

How is it that we each hear them in our own language to which we were born? Parthians and Medes and Elamites, and residents of Mesopotamia, Judea and Cappadocia, Pontus and Asia, Phrygia and Pamphylia, Egypt and the districts of Libya around Cyrene, and visitors from Rome, both Jews and proselytes, Cretans and Arabs—we hear them in our own tongues speaking of the mighty deeds of God. (Acts 2:8–11)

The message that was shared by the believers on the day of Pentecost with those on the streets dealt with "the mighty deeds of God." If evangelism is *the presentation of the good news of Jesus' death for our sin and of His burial and resurrection according to the Scriptures in an understandable way that calls for a response of faith and repentance*, then what the 120 were doing on this day is what we would call "broad seed sowing" rather than direct evangelism. Later in Acts 2 Peter will clearly present the good news of Jesus' death and resurrection based on the authority of Scripture, and he will give a clear opportunity for people to respond to the message, but the text doesn't indicate that the 120 were doing this. The text simply says they were "speaking of the mighty deeds of God."

The broad sowing of the Word of God in people's lives is good preparation for evangelism.

Jesus taught the parable of the sower, in which the sower went out to broadcast, or scatter, seeds. The seed was broadly sown, causing it to land in different places. The seed sown in Jesus' parable was "the word of God" (Luke 8:11)—not a specific gospel message but a broad sowing of the Word of God. This seems consistent with the work of the 120 in Acts 2. The broad sowing of the Word of God can be considered good preparation for specific evangelism. Romans 10:17 makes clear that "faith comes from hearing, and hearing by the word of Christ."

Church planters today find that broad seed sowing through Scripture distribution, gospel radio broadcasts, videos or movies of Bible stories, Scripture in newspaper ads, or websites containing Scripture can be excellent preparation for future evangelism. In a project called Operation GO, teams distribute gospel portions door to door, preferably alongside national believers who will return to interested families for church planting. In other parts of the world, believers respond to local people's hospitality by sharing tea with them for several hours and then asking for permission to show them gratitude with a special gift: God's Word. Broad seed sowing is pictured in Acts 2 and is practiced today.

Beginning Where People Are and Then Going to the Cross

They all continued in amazement and great perplexity, saying to one another, "What does this mean?" But others were mocking and saying, "They are full of sweet wine."

But Peter, taking his stand with the eleven, raised his voice and declared to them: "Men of Judea and all you who live in Jerusalem, let this be known to you and give heed to my words. For these men are not drunk, as you suppose, for it is only the third hour of the day; but this is what was spoken of through the prophet Joel: 'And it shall be in the last days,' God says, 'that I will pour forth of My Spirit on all mankind; and your sons and your daughters shall prophesy, and your young men shall see visions, and your old men shall dream dreams; even on My bondslaves, both men and women, I will in those days pour forth of My Spirit and they shall prophesy. And I will grant wonders in the sky above and signs on the earth below, blood, and fire, and vapor of smoke. The sun will be turned into darkness and the moon into blood, before the great and glorious day of the Lord shall come. And it shall be that everyone who calls on the name of the Lord will be saved.'

Men of Israel, listen to these words: Jesus the Nazarene, a man attested to you by God with miracles and wonders and signs which God performed through Him in your midst, just as you yourselves know—this Man, delivered over by the predetermined plan and foreknowledge of God, you nailed to a cross by the hands of godless men and put Him to death. But God raised Him up again, putting an end to the agony of death, since it was impossible for Him to be held in its power. For David says of Him, 'I saw the Lord always in my presence; for He is at my right hand, so that I will not be shaken. Therefore my heart was glad and my tongue exulted; moreover my flesh also will live in hope; because You will not abandon my soul to Hades, nor allow Your Holy One to undergo decay. You have made known to me the ways of life; you will make me full of gladness with your presence.'

Brethren, I may confidently say to you regarding the patriarch David that he both died and was buried, and his tomb is with us to this day. And so, because he was a prophet and knew that God had sworn to him an oath to seat one of his descendants on his throne, he looked ahead and spoke of the resurrection of the Christ, that He was neither abandoned to Hades, nor did His flesh suffer decay. This Jesus God raised up again, to which we are all witnesses. Therefore having been exalted to the right hand of God, and having received from the Father the promise of the Holy Spirit, He has poured forth this which you both see and hear. For it was not David who ascended into heaven, but he himself says: 'The Lord said to my Lord, "Sit at my right hand, until I make your enemies a footstool for your feet."'

Therefore let all the house of Israel know for certain that God has made Him both Lord and Christ—this Jesus whom you crucified." (Acts 2:12–36)

As the crowd responded with amazement and perplexity to the 120 sharing the wonders of God in their heart languages, some began to mock the believers, accusing them of being "full of sweet wine." Peter picked up on that very expression to begin speaking: "These men are not drunk, as you suppose, for it is only the third hour of the day; but this is what was spoken of through the prophet." A very natural way to share the gospel is to listen carefully to what people say and to use some part of their conversation to segue to the gospel. Start with where they are and then go to the cross! Peter started with where the people were, and then he went to the cross and the resurrection.

It is the Holy Spirit who convicts and draws people.

An emphasis on the cross and the resurrection of Jesus is seen throughout the book of Acts.[10] According to First Corinthians 15, the gospel message is that Jesus Christ died for our sins and was buried and raised from the dead according to the Scriptures (see 15:1, 3–4). It is good to talk about God's love or to share thoughts about various scriptural topics, but if those who have been sent out do not talk to people about the cross and resurrection, the people listening did not hear the good news![11] When Peter preached on the day of Pentecost, half his sermon contained quotes from the Old Testament. Just as it was for Peter, the authority for the gospel message today is the Word of God.

Conviction, Repentance and Faith

Now when they heard this, they were pierced to the heart, and said to Peter and the rest of the apostles, "Brethren, what shall we do?" Peter said to them, "Repent, and each of you be baptized in the name of Jesus Christ for the forgiveness of your sins; and you will receive the gift of the Holy Spirit . . ." And all those who had believed were together and had all things in common. (Acts 2:37–38, 44)

Those who responded positively to Peter's message were challenged to repent and believe the good news. They were

motivated because they were "pierced to the heart." It is the
work of the Holy Spirit, as we read in John 16:8–11, to convict
the world of sin, righteousness and judgment. It is God who
draws people to Himself. Jesus said, "No one can come to Me
unless the Father who sent Me draws him" (6:44), and later
He promised, referring to His death on the cross, "I, if I am
lifted up from the earth, will draw all men to Myself" (12:32).
The church planter, or sent-out one (a term we will discuss in
chapter 6 of this book),[12] is to clearly present the gospel, but
then must also recognize that it is the Holy Spirit who convicts and draws people to respond.

The twofold response that Peter calls for, repentance and
belief, matches the command of Jesus after He preached: "Repent and believe in the gospel" (Mark 1:14–15). Peter ends
his second sermon in Acts with the same command, "Therefore repent" (3:19). In response to the council's questions in
Acts 5, Peter explains that God has exalted Jesus to His right
hand and that the appropriate response is repentance (see
5:31). Paul continues the same emphasis on repentance that
we find in Peter's preaching. At the end of his third missionary journey, Paul met with the elders, or overseers, from the
church at Ephesus and described his ministry as "testifying
to both Jews and Greeks of repentance toward God and faith
in our Lord Jesus Christ" (20:21). Repentance and faith are
the responses to the gospel most often called for in the book
of Acts.

Baptism

> So then, those who had received his word were baptized; and
> that day there were added about three thousand souls. (Acts
> 2:41)

Just as Peter calls for response to his first sermon in Acts 2 by commanding the hearers to repent, he also commands them to be baptized in the name of Jesus Christ. It had not been many days since Peter had heard the Lord Jesus say that all authority had been given to Him and that with this authority Peter and every follower of Jesus were to make disciples of all ethnicities, "baptizing them in the name of the Father and the Son and the Holy Spirit" (Matt. 28:19–20). Baptism was a central part of the believers' commission. It was part of Peter's marching orders. The command was clear to Peter, and he made it clear to those listening on the day of Pentecost: "Those who had received his word were baptized; and that day there were added about three thousand souls." The call for response was clear, and many responded.

While there is no command in the book of Acts as to when new believers are to be baptized, the immediacy with which baptism took place in this instance is striking. Those who repented, believed and were baptized "were added," a phrase that is amplified in Acts 2:47 with the words "to their number."[13] Baptism following repentance, which followed faith, or believing, was the way in which new believers became part of the church.

Along with the commands to repent and be baptized, Peter added an important promise: "You will receive the gift of the Holy Spirit" (2:38). As has been noted above, the role of the Holy Spirit is key and is emphasized in the book of Acts. Here we learn that the Holy Spirit is not for some select group in the church or just for the leaders. The next verse emphasizes that the promise of the Spirit is for these new believers "and for all who are far off, as many as the Lord our God will call to Himself" (Acts 2:39). This matches what Paul teaches in Romans 8:9, where his readers are told that "the Spirit of God dwells in [them]" and that anyone who does not have the Spirit does not belong to Christ.

If church planters mistakenly believe that they are the only ones in whom God's presence dwells, they will often make their work dependent on themselves. The biblical truth that every true believer has God living inside him or her allows the church planter to have confidence in God who indwells each new believer.

Overview of the Jerusalem Church

The Jerusalem church was birthed in prayer, followed by the people responding to a God-controlled event that led to broad sharing by all the believers in the heart languages of their hearers. When Peter presented the gospel on the authority of the Scriptures, the Holy Spirit drew people to salvation and filled each new believer. The apostles then discipled those who believed, which led to a healthy, vibrant church.

This pattern set the stage for the churches to come in the book of Acts.

Notes:
- It seems as if God was setting a model for church planting through Peter & the church in Jerusalem.
- an important concept that is found in the church in Jerusalem, was meeting people where they were at but also loving them not judging them.

Notes cont:
- Peter was bold in his love
but also bold in what ~~the~~
he preached.
- Peter spoke the truth and
through the Holy Spirit tackled
the hearts of the people.
· not because it was
something they wanted to
hear - but it was something
they needed to hear.

2

THE CHURCH IN JERUSALEM, PART 2

Acts 2:42–6:7

The Jerusalem church had now begun. Immediately following its narrative of the beginning of the first church, the book of Acts goes on to describe the activities of the new church, giving us the model of a healthy church.

Because a healthy church leads to growth, the chapters immediately following the description of the new church detail the spread of the Jerusalem church into the regions around the city. In this chapter we will take a look at both the characteristics of the healthy Jerusalem church and the multiplication of that church.

*A sound scriptural foundation can produce
a non-foreign church in every culture.*

As we look first at the behavior of the brand-new Jerusalem believers, we discover five major characteristics of this church: discipleship, fellowship, worship, ministry, and evangelism and missions. These characteristics define a healthy church, both then and now, and they are one of the common threads that will appear throughout the book of Acts in all nine of the new church plants.

Church planters today will do well to build the biblical characteristics discovered here into the DNA of a new church and to intentionally leave out traditions that are not distinctly taught in Scripture. This is particularly true when working in an unfamiliar culture. Traditions not clearly taught in Scripture may work well when we are planting a new church among our *own* people group in our *own* city, but in a culture unfamiliar to the church planter, they can often make the church look foreign to the new believers. Because God's Word fits every culture in every generation, a clearly scriptural foundation can produce a native church in every culture.

Discipleship: The Apostles' Teaching

> They were continually devoting themselves to the apostles' teaching. (Acts 2:42)

---

*The disciples taught the new believers,
just as the Great Commission commanded.*

The description of the new church states that the brand-new believers "were continually devoting themselves" to several things, the first of which was the apostles' teaching. The Greek noun for "teaching" comes from the verb used in the Great Commission: "teaching them to obey" (Matt. 28:20, NIV). The apostles had baptized the new believers just as the commission commanded, and now they were teaching the fledgling church just like the commission commanded.

While the Jerusalem church had the apostles in their midst and could devote themselves to the apostles' teaching face to face, churches in later generations have devoted themselves to the apostles' teaching as it is recorded in the New Testament. Commitment to the Scriptures on the part of the church planter is foundational to planting healthy churches. Discipleship of the believers in the new church, based on God's Word, is of primary importance.

Fellowship

> They were continually devoting themselves to . . . fellowship. (Acts 2:42)

The Jerusalem church further demonstrated their health by their fellowship with one another. This fellowship[1] is an extremely important aspect of a healthy church. Jesus said, "By this all men will know that you are My disciples, if you have love for one another" (John 13:35). The way believers relate to one another inside the church will authenticate the message they proclaim. If those outside the church do not see love inside it, they will be less inclined to believe the message.

The way believers relate to one another inside the church will authenticate the message they proclaim outside the church.

Paul instructs the new churches in Galatia to pay attention to their witness toward outsiders in a verse that seems a little unusual at first: "So then, while we have opportunity, let us do good to all people, and especially to those who are of the household of the faith" (Gal. 6:10). We would expect a command to do good to the lost, to those outside the church. But the verse emphasizes the opposite because the fellowship inside a church is immensely important and an indicator of its health.

Worship: the Lord's Supper

> They were continually devoting themselves to . . . the breaking of bread. (Acts 2:42)

The believers in Jerusalem continually devoted themselves to "the breaking of bread." While at first glance this phrase may be understood as an expression of the fellowship just mentioned, it instead seems to be introducing a distinct element of a healthy church—one that we know as the Lord's Supper.[2]

The Lord Jesus commanded two ordinances, both of which are woven throughout the New Testament: baptism and the Lord's Supper.[3] Baptism is pictured throughout Acts as the manner in which new believers give public testimony of their new faith and repentance. The Lord's Supper is also pictured as a normal part of the worship of the churches. Paul writes to the Corinthian church, one of the churches in Acts that we will examine later, "Is not the cup of blessing which we bless a sharing in the blood of Christ? Is not the bread which we break a sharing in the body of Christ?" (1 Cor. 10:16), stating the sharing of the cup and the breaking of bread as the normal practice of the churches. The inclusion of the Lord's Supper in the worship services of new churches today provides beautiful depth, and perhaps solemnity, to their worship.

Worship: Prayer

> They were continually devoting themselves to . . . prayer.
> (Acts 2:42)

Finally, according to Acts 2:42, the members of the church devoted themselves to prayer. We have noted how the apostles and those who began the church were committed to prayer. Now we find their disciples praying.

It is typical that new churches will practice what their church planters modeled more than what their church planters talked about. The disciples asked Jesus to teach them to pray on one of the many occasions when they observed Him praying (see Luke 11:1). The example of the church planters often becomes the DNA of the new church.

Ministry: Generous Giving

> Everyone kept feeling a sense of awe; and many wonders and signs were taking place through the apostles. And all those who had believed were together and had all things in common; and they began selling their property and possessions and were sharing them with all, as anyone might have need. (Acts 2:43–45)

---

*New churches in the book of Acts practiced
stewardship from the beginning.*

The new church in Jerusalem was characterized by generous giving to meet the needs of the body. A fuller description of this giving is found in Acts 4 and also in Acts 5, which describes the challenge to giving presented by Ananias and

Sapphira's deception. The practice of the Jerusalem church is best described as generous giving rather than as some form of communism, which we deduce from Peter's words to the couple in Acts 5:4: "While it remained unsold, did it not remain your own? And after it was sold, was it not under your control?" In the new church, property belonged to its owners, and giving was under their control.

If we let Scripture interpret Scripture, we conclude that the church practiced extremely generous giving for the purpose of meeting needs. This pattern of new churches practicing stewardship from the outset is found in numerous places in the New Testament. The new church at Antioch collected an offering for those facing famine in another region (see Acts 11:28–30). The new church in Philippi sent an offering to support missionary work shortly after they became a church (see Phil. 4:15–16).

The Jerusalem church met daily for worship.

The Philippian church is noted for giving "according to their ability, and beyond their ability" (2 Cor. 8:3), even though their own financial condition at the time is described as "deep poverty" (8:2). This is an important corrective for church planters who do not teach stewardship because their new churches are "too poor." The Holy Spirit provided us a specific example of generous giving through a new church that was in deep poverty. Generous giving by new Christians is the example found in the healthy church in Jerusalem.

Worship: Praise

> Day by day continuing with one mind in the temple, and breaking bread from house to house, they were taking their meals together with gladness and sincerity of heart, praising God and having favor with all the people. And the Lord was adding to their number day by day those who were being saved. (Acts 2:46–47)

The Jerusalem church met daily for worship. The word translated "praising" in Acts 2:47 is the same word used of the angels singing before the shepherds at the birth of Jesus (see Luke 2:13). The New Testament teaches believers to use "psalms and hymns and spiritual songs, singing and making melody with [our] heart to the Lord" (Eph. 5:19). Teaching, prayer and the Lord's Supper, which we saw in verse 42, were likely part of the Jerusalem church's worship services.

Evangelism and Missions

> The Lord was adding to their number day by day those who were being saved. (Acts 2:47)

Although three thousand people believed and were baptized the day the Jerusalem church was born (see 2:41), the growth of the new church was just beginning. "And the Lord was adding to their number day by day those who were being saved." Assuming that we are to use Acts 2 as a starting point, or as our context, for understanding what this verse might mean, the Lord's adding apparently included bold sharing, the presentation of the gospel, the Holy Spirit's drawing and people's response of faith and repentance. The Lord's daily adding matches the timing mentioned in Acts 5:42: "And every day, in the temple and from house to house, they kept right on

teaching and preaching Jesus as the Christ." Growth is clearly
pictured as normal in the book of Acts.[4]

Meeting Locations

> Day by day continuing with one mind in the temple, and
> breaking bread from house to house. (Acts 2:46)

The new church continued meeting in two locales: in the
temple and from house to house. Several types of locations are
mentioned for meetings in the book of Acts: the giant temple
constructed for the worship of Almighty God (see 2:46; 5:42),
a riverside (see 16:13), "in the market place" (17:17) and "in
the school of Tyrannus" (19:9); all these kinds of settings are
used by churches and church planters today (church buildings,
parks, storefronts and school buildings). Yet the location mentioned most often in the book of Acts as a place for believers
to meet is in homes (see 2:46; 5:42; 10:22; 12:12; 16:32, 40;
18:7; 20:20).

This matches what we see in the rest of the New Testament. Romans 16:5 tells us of a church in Rome that met in
Aquila and Priscilla's home. The first letter to the Corinthians, written several years before Romans, was written from
Ephesus (see 1 Cor. 16:8) and mentions a church in Ephesus
that also met in the home of Aquila and Priscilla when they
lived in that city (see 16:19).[5] We read of a church that met in
Nympha's house (see Col. 4:15) and one that met in Archip-
pus' house (see Philem. 1:2). In the New Testament the most
common place for a church to meet was a home.[6] That pattern
began in the healthy Jerusalem church described in Acts 2.

The description of the Jerusalem church found in the closing verses of Acts 2 provides the church planter a model or

example of what churches, as the body of Christ, should practice. The goal is for new churches to be healthy, and this example serves as a guide for what a healthy church is and does.

Persecution as Normal

> As they were speaking to the people, the priests and the cap-
> tain of the temple guard and the Sadducees came up to them,
> being greatly disturbed because they were teaching the people
> and proclaiming in Jesus the resurrection from the dead. And
> they laid hands on them and put them in jail until the next
> day, for it was already evening. But many of those who had
> heard the message believed; and the number of the men came
> to be about five thousand. (Acts 4:1–4)

We have looked at the beginning of the Jerusalem church
and at the characteristics that demonstrated that the church
was healthy. Now we will consider the passages in Acts that
describe the growth of the Jerusalem church. In them we will
find some of the unique insights that the book of Acts presents as we examine the first church in Jerusalem.

One of the things evident in the new church was that
signs and wonders were taking place through the apostles
(see 2:43), an example of which was the healing of a lame
beggar at the entrance to the temple (see 3:1–4:31).[7] Peter
appeared to follow the example of Jesus, who had said to the
man who had been ill for thirty-eight years, "Get up, pick up
your pallet and walk" (John 5:8). On this occasion in Acts 3,
it appears that the man who was healed may have come to
faith, because he responded with praise to God (see 3:8), but
Acts never specifically states that anyone who was healed
or had a demon cast out came to faith. Many sent-out ones
today apply Jesus' words to heal the sick (see Luke 9:2; 10:9)

by praying for people's healing, deliverance and wholeness in Jesus' name. Others take Jesus' description of the Good Samaritan as an indication that they should bind up wounds and provide medical attention.[8]

As a result of the lame man's healing and the Jewish opposition to it, Peter and John were arrested and put in prison, a very common event in the book of Acts. We read of believers in jail or prison or held captive in twelve chapters in Acts.[9] If we add chapters 6 and 7, where Stephen is before the council, and chapter 27, where Paul is under Roman guard, more than half the chapters in the book of Acts describe believers as in prison or being detained.

More than half the chapters in Acts describe believers as in prison or being detained.

Persecution is not to be seen as unusual for followers of Christ. Peter writes, "Beloved, do not be surprised at the fiery ordeal among you, which comes upon you for your testing, as though some strange thing were happening to you" (1 Pet. 4:12). Paul writes that persecution will be the experience of all: "Indeed, all who desire to live godly in Christ Jesus will be persecuted" (2 Tim. 3:12). Jesus Himself described tribulation as normal but also promised us victory when we go through it: "In the world you have tribulation, but take courage; I have overcome the world" (John 16:33). The church planter should prepare new believers to assume that persecution is normal and train them to walk in victory in the midst of that persecution.

Instead of being intimidated by the possibility of persecution, the Jerusalem church prayed for boldness,[10] and as a
consequence of being filled with the Holy Spirit, the believers continued sharing. Remember that every member of the
church-planting team, the 120, had been filled with the Spirit
(see Acts 2:4) and that all who had responded to the gospel
with faith and repentance had also been promised "the gift
of the Holy Spirit" (2:38). In Acts 4:31 we read that "they
were all filled with the Holy Spirit," and the result is that they
spoke "the word of God with boldness."[11]

New Leaders, or Workers

Now at this time while the disciples were increasing in
number, a complaint arose on the part of the Hellenistic
Jews against the native Hebrews, because their widows were
being overlooked in the daily serving of food. So the twelve
summoned the congregation of the disciples and said, "It
is not desirable for us to neglect the word of God in order to serve tables. Therefore, brethren, select from among
you seven men of good reputation, full of the Spirit and of
wisdom, whom we may put in charge of this task. But we
will devote ourselves to prayer and to the ministry of the
word." The statement found approval with the whole congregation; and they chose Stephen, a man full of faith and
of the Holy Spirit, and Philip, Prochorus, Nicanor, Timon,
Parmenas and Nicolas, a proselyte from Antioch. And these
they brought before the apostles; and after praying, they
laid their hands on them.

The word of God kept on spreading; and the number of
the disciples continued to increase greatly in Jerusalem, and a
great many of the priests were becoming obedient to the faith.
(Acts 6:1–7)

When Paul writes to the church at Philippi, he mentions two groups of leaders: overseers and deacons (see Phil. 1:1). These same two groups are discussed in First Timothy 3. In Acts 20 and in First Peter 5, overseers are referred to as elders and also as shepherds (the word *overseer* can also be translated "bishop"). Overseers, or elders or shepherds, are those who pastor the church.[12] Acts 6, as we noted at the beginning of this section, describes how a second type of servant[13] was added to the church's leadership when the believers chose seven men to distribute food. These deacons were added in the Jerusalem church when there was a need for them. A church planter need not place structure on a new church that it is not yet ready to support, but the New Testament example is that new churches are to have leadership.

Leaders in the new church came from within the church.

It is important to note that these deacons came from within the local group, a normal pattern throughout the book of Acts, and that their qualifications were spiritual in nature. The apostles instructed the church here in Acts 6:3, "Select from among you." At the end of Paul's first missionary journey, he and Barnabas "appointed elders for them in every church" (14:23). The text implies that these elders came from within the churches. On one occasion we are told of a leader (not one of the church planters) coming from a place other than the church,[14] but the pattern appears to be that leadership comes from within the church body. In the New Testament passages about spiritual gifts, we are told that the Holy Spirit gifts some believers as teachers (see Rom. 12:7; 1 Cor. 12:28), and in Ephesians 4 we are told that He gives pastor-teachers to the church to equip the body (see 4:11–13). In Acts 6, First Timothy 3 and Titus 1, the qualifications for leaders in the church deal with character and spiritual maturity.

Acts 7 and 8 describe how well these leaders, Stephen in particular, did in the face of persecution. Persecution against them resulted in the church's first martyr—and also in the gospel being extended to the Samaritans and to the African continent. This pattern of members from the Jerusalem church evangelizing wherever they went is continued in Acts 11, where they also planted the next church in Antioch. This church in Antioch was then used to start other churches that would spread the gospel throughout entire regions. The church planter's goal is to start churches that will start other churches, leading to multiplication like that pictured in the book of Acts beginning with this first church, the church in Jerusalem.

Overview of Characteristics and Growth of the Jerusalem Church

The Jerusalem church provides us the description of a healthy church: It was characterized by discipleship, fellowship, worship, ministry, and evangelism and missions. Leaders were added to the church from the congregation. Persecution followed. The gospel spread, leading to a church that planted churches.

Parts of this Jerusalem experience will be repeated over and over again, as we will see, in the narrative of Acts.

- the church in Jerusalem
did things that churchs tend
to not do at all.

- there was an order put
in place in the church.

- it wasn't much different
from what they were already
doing.

3

THE CHURCH IN ANTIOCH

Acts 8:1–13:4

As we have seen, the early chapters of the book of Acts describe the beginning of the Jerusalem church. That healthy church probably planted "the churches of Judea" (Gal. 1:22) and those in Samaria (see Acts 9:31), although we are not given the details of these church plants.

The next church plant that Luke, under the inspiration of the Holy Spirit, chooses to tell us about in his narrative of the Acts of the Apostles is the church in Antioch, which was in Syria, north of Israel. We will follow Luke's account in Acts 8–13, examining this church plant as well as the circumstances that led to its birthing.

The Gospel Goes to Samaria and Beyond

Saul was in hearty agreement with putting [Stephen] to death. And on that day a great persecution began against the church in Jerusalem, and they were all scattered throughout the regions of Judea and Samaria, except the apostles. Some devout men buried Stephen, and made loud lamentation over him. But Saul began ravaging the church, entering house after house, and dragging off men and women, he would put them in prison.

47

Therefore, those who had been scattered went about preaching the word. Philip went down to the city of Samaria and began proclaiming Christ to them. (Acts 8:1–5)

Sound contextualization: those portions of the culture inconsistent with God's Word are not to be tolerated.

The church plant in Antioch was prefaced by a negative. The stoning death of Stephen (see 6:8–7:60), one of the seven who had been selected as a deacon in the Jerusalem church, led to persecution of the growing church. This in turn caused the new believers from the Jerusalem church to be scattered.

Philip, another of the seven deacons, took the gospel to the city of Samaria, and men and women in that place believed and were baptized. Peter and John were soon sent by the Jerusalem church to join him; it appears that these two were involved in the believers receiving the Spirit for the sake of unifying the church as one.

While in Samaria Peter and John also confronted Simon, a magician who had believed. In Simon's life before Christ, he would have offered money to buy new magic tricks. Now he attempted to bring his old way of life into the new life as a Christian by offering the disciples money in exchange for the ability to endow people with the Holy Spirit, as God had done through Peter and John (see 8:18–19). The apostles were faced with a contextualization challenge—a question as to how they would minister the gospel within this particular cultural situation. Would this practice of using money in order to gain prestige or influence be allowed among the believers? The apostles clearly demonstrated sound contextualization:

they declared that those portions of the culture or of a new believer's past that were inconsistent with God's Word and ways would not be tolerated in the new community of faith (see Acts 8:20).[1]

While we are not told specifically where in Samaria churches were planted, Acts 9 tells us that the church throughout all Samaria was being built up (see 9:31). From there it spilled over to other places. When Philip was instructed by an angel to go to a desert road south of Jerusalem, he immediately left the revival in Samaria and obeyed.

Naturally, wherever God places sent-out ones, He has already been working in the lives of individuals who need to hear the gospel. ~ true

---

In this story we see another principle at work: naturally, wherever God places sent-out ones, He has already been working in the lives of individuals who need to hear the gospel.[2] Such was the case with the man Philip encountered on the road: the Word of God had been sown[3] in the heart of this Ethiopian eunuch, who, as he rode in his chariot, was reading from the part of Isaiah 53 that talks about Jesus' substitutionary death. Starting with this passage, Philip preached Jesus to him. Then they went down into the water, and the Ethiopian eunuch was baptized (see Acts 8:32–38).

Here we see a pattern that God seems to repeat today. Someone receives a copy of God's Word, he or she starts reading the Bible, and when the worker shows up, the person is ready to listen and believe. The Scripture text does not tell us, but one wonders if this story of Philip and the Ethiopian eunuch is not how the first church in sub-Saharan Africa was begun. After the eunuch's baptism Philip was snatched away by the Spirit (see Acts 8:39) and later went to Caesarea, where we encounter him again in Acts 21. It appears that Philip had a major part in the gospel being taken to two new places, and then he settled down to life in one place.[4]

A Chief Persecutor Comes to Faith

> Now Saul, still breathing threats and murder against the disciples of the Lord, went to the high priest, and asked for letters from him to the synagogues at Damascus, so that if he found any belonging to the Way, both men and women, he might bring them bound to Jerusalem. As he was traveling, it happened that he was approaching Damascus, and suddenly a light from heaven flashed around him; and he fell to the ground and heard a voice saying to him, "Saul, Saul, why are you persecuting Me?" And he said, "Who are You, Lord?" And He said, "I am Jesus whom you are persecuting, but get up and enter the city, and it will be told you what you must do." (9:1–6)

Those from the Jerusalem church who were scattered in response to Stephen's persecution also went further north to Antioch; but before we get there, we want to look at Acts 9, which describes God's working not just with those who were persecuted or scattered but with the chief persecutor himself.

Saul of Tarsus (who will begin to use his Greek name, Paul, in Acts 13) was present the day Stephen died, and in the wake of that tragedy, Saul became the chief persecutor of the church (see 26:9–11). As he traveled north to Damascus one day in his zeal to persecute the church, the Lord Jesus appeared to him on the road. This one who had been wreaking havoc in the churches was no match for the risen Lord. Saul was blinded by a light that was brighter than the noonday sun, and shortly afterward, when God sent the prophet Ananias to visit with him, Saul responded in faith (see Acts 9:10–18). Once again we find that God had been at work in an individual's heart before His servant, in this case Ananias, arrived on the scene. The pattern of Acts 9 resembles that of Acts 8 (and that of God's working today): wherever God sends a worker, He has already been at work preparing people to believe.

Ananias baptized Saul, who immediately began sharing the gospel in Damascus (see 9:19–20). From there he went to Arabia and later returned to Damascus (see Gal. 1:17). Three years after his conversion (see 1:18), when "the Jews plotted together to do away with him" (Acts 9:23), Saul was let down in a basket over the city wall, and made his way to Jerusalem. There he attempted to associate with the disciples, but they were afraid of him (see 9:26), and he did not have much success until Barnabas took him to the apostles and told of his transformed life (see 9:27).

"The workers are in the harvest."

Notice that this powerful new worker came from the harvest of new Christians. A saying that my colleagues and I often repeat, "The workers are in the harvest," was true in Saul's situation.

One of the most significant things that Barnabas, the established Christian, did was to connect Saul, a relatively new believer, with other believers and to open doors for him. Notice also that God used Barnabas' God-given identity in this incident. Barnabas' real name was Joseph, but he had been given the nickname "son of encouragement" (*Barnabas*) because he was always encouraging people (see Acts 4:36–37). Encouragement means "called alongside of,"[5] and that is exactly what Barnabas was: he was a man who came alongside the new worker and connected him with leaders in the church. God normally uses sent-out ones in a way that is consistent with the gifts and talents that He has given them.

Now that we have looked at the persecution and scattering of the Jerusalem believers as well as how Barnabas met Saul, we are ready to look at the new church plant in Antioch.

Ordinary Believers Started Churches

> So those who were scattered because of the persecution that occurred in connection with Stephen made their way to Phoenicia and Cyprus and Antioch, speaking the word to no one except to Jews alone. (11:19)

Ordinary believers started a church
where there was not one.

Some of the believers from the Jerusalem church who had been scattered by the persecution that arose from Stephen's martyrdom traveled further north than Samaria. Some reached the coastal region of Phoenicia, others reached the island of Cyprus, and still others reached the city of Antioch. In contrast to the case of Philip, Scripture does not record the names of these believers. They are not described as leaders or as specially trained or gifted. Through these unnamed, ordinary believers, the Lord built His church. Throughout church history the Lord has continued to use ordinary believers who have gone where there is no church to begin new local churches in those places.

My father, Eurvin Smith, was a deacon in my home church as I grew up. He was a commercial carpenter who instilled in me a love for God's Word by faithfully reading through the Bible year after year. When he and my mother, Alene, moved our family to a community east of Tulsa, Oklahoma, that had no Baptist church, they met with a couple of other interested families and began the church I grew up in. They were ordinary Christians who started a church when they moved to a place where there was not one. They followed in a long history of believers doing this, a history that goes back to these nameless individuals in Acts 11. Church planting, in the book of Acts, is not just for missionaries or pastors. Church planting is for any Christian.

Sharing with Greeks

> So those who were scattered because of the persecution that occurred in connection with Stephen made their way to Phoenicia and Cyprus and Antioch, speaking the word to no one except to Jews alone. But there were some of them, men of Cyprus and Cyrene, who came to Antioch and began speaking to the Greeks also, preaching the Lord Jesus. And the hand of the Lord was with them, and a large number who believed turned to the Lord. (Acts 11:19–21)

Most of the people going out from the Jerusalem church shared the gospel only with Jews, but Jesus had made it clear that this was not His desire (see Matt. 28:19). Perhaps these believers were intimidated by others, or perhaps they were more comfortable with their own race. We are told at the beginning of Acts 8 that these men and women left Jerusalem, so they were gone before the Jerusalem church started sharing with the Samaritans (see Acts 8:4–25) and with the Gentiles (see 10:1–11:18). Perhaps they shared only with the Jews because *that is what they had watched the apostles do.* The text leaves us with the possibility that the apostles had modeled limited obedience to the Great Commission and so inserted that model into the DNA of the believers. That is a sobering thought for church planters, because if we neglect part of or add to New Testament Christianity, our example may well be followed by new believers. That said, the reason for the believers sharing only with the Jews is not given, just the limits of their sharing.

Sound contextualization: incorporating and/or redeeming those aspects of culture commanded in or consistent with Scripture.

"But there were some of them" who had been scattered from the Jerusalem church who began to share with Greeks also. As they began sharing the gospel with this new group, they were "preaching the Lord Jesus." Up to this point in the book of Acts, it has been more typical for the believers to talk about *Jesus Christ*, or Jesus the Messiah, when sharing with the lost.[6] But as believers shared the gospel with the Greeks in Antioch, they did not begin by talking about a Messiah that the Greeks were not expecting. They spoke instead of the *Lord* Jesus.[7] The word *lord* was used in those days for other gods and also for the Caesar.

Of course, Jesus is both Messiah and Lord: both terms are completely accurate. But we can adjust the way in which we present the truth in order to communicate better to a new people group. This use by the believers of the word *lord* is an example of the positive side of contextualization. Not only does sound contextualization require that we reject those things in a culture that are inconsistent with Scripture (remember the discussion of Simon the magician above), it also requires that we incorporate and/or redeem those aspects of a culture that are commanded in or consistent with Scripture.

A Large Number Believed

> And the hand of the Lord was with them, and a large number who believed turned to the Lord. The news about them reached the ears of the church at Jerusalem, and they sent Barnabas off to Antioch. Then when he arrived and witnessed the grace of God, he rejoiced and began to encourage them all with resolute heart to remain true to the Lord; for he was a good man, and full of the Holy Spirit and of faith. And considerable numbers were brought to the Lord. (Acts 11:21–24)

A large number of people in Phoenicia and Cyprus and Antioch believed and turned to the Lord because "the hand of the Lord was with" the apostles. The church planter must always remember that salvation is the work of God. His or her part is to be obedient, proclaim the gospel and faithfully do what the Word of God teaches sent-out ones to do. We remember from Acts 2 that Peter faithfully preached the gospel, but it was the work of the Holy Spirit to pierce the hearts of the listeners (see 2:37).

The church in Jerusalem heard about what was going on in the places where these new believers had gone, and the leaders sent Barnabas to Antioch. When Barnabas, the encourager, saw what God was doing there, he began "to encourage [the believers] with resolute heart to remain true to the Lord" (Acts 11:23). The church had sent the right person—the person with the right gifts—to Antioch.

---

*Barnabas was a good man,
full of the Holy Spirit and of faith..*

Acts 11:24 describes further attributes of Barnabas: "He was a good man, and full of the Holy Spirit and of faith." Character matters—he was a good man. The book of Acts places a major emphasis on the work of the Holy Spirit.[8] Workers must remember that they are commanded by Scripture to "be filled with the Spirit" (Eph. 5:18), a present-tense command referring to continual action. The power for sent-out ones comes from the Holy Spirit (see Acts 1:8). Barnabas also is described as a person "full of faith."[9] Faith is vital in church planting. We are told in Hebrews 11:6 that "without faith it is impossible to please" God. Jesus' words to two blind men underscore the importance of going out to share the gospel with faith: "It shall be done to you according to your faith" (Matt. 9:29). Sent-out ones go to minister believing that God's Word is truth and that every clear promise God gave will come true. They also prayerfully seek God's will in their situation and pray in faith, believing that what He has said, He is able to do.

Those who had responded to the gospel before Barnabas arrived included "a large number who believed" (Acts 11:21). After he arrived, Scripture records, "considerable numbers were brought to the Lord" (11:24). The pattern of large numerical growth seen in the Jerusalem church (see 2:41; 4:4) also played out in Antioch.

These passages, however, present me with a dilemma. I am extremely grateful for the growth that has taken place in the areas where my wife and I have served, but our experience does not completely match these passages. While it is true that these narrative passages do not promise that everyone will see these same results, I want to be careful not to explain away Scripture based on what I have seen and thus make my own experience, or that of anyone else, the norm in place of Scripture.

In the parable of the sower, Jesus pictured some of the sower's seed falling on good soil. Good seed in good soil produced vastly different responses (sometimes a hundredfold, sometimes sixty, sometimes thirty), but it always resulted in multiplication (see Matt. 13:8). On several occasions Paul asked people to pray for him or for his ministry team, and he listed great prayer requests that can be used for sent-out ones of any age.[10] We can call these missionary prayers. We are to pray, as Paul requested the early believers to pray, "that the word of the Lord will spread rapidly" (2 Thess. 3:1). Instead of explaining away the Word of God when it pictures something different from my experience, I want to hold God's Word as my norm for faith and practice and continue to ask Him to bring it to pass.

A Year Teaching the Church

And [Barnabas] left for Tarsus to look for Saul; and when he had found him, he brought him to Antioch. And for an entire year they met with the church and taught considerable numbers; and the disciples were first called Christians in Antioch. (Acts 11:25–26)

Barnabas left Antioch, went to Tarsus to find Saul and brought him back to help in the work. We have already noticed Barnabas' previous powerful work in connecting Saul with other believers when Saul arrived in Jerusalem three years after his salvation. Since that time Paul had been preaching for nearly ten years in the regions of Syria and Cilicia (see Gal. 1:18, 21–2:1). Now Barnabas again connected Saul with other believers, this time with the new church in Antioch.

When we realize how significant the Antioch church became in Paul's life (we will see this church's major role in sending Paul out as a church planter later in this chapter), we recognize the importance of Barnabas encouraging Paul and connecting him with these believers. For some sent-out ones, their greatest ministry will be in connecting national believers with each other, which will enable them to accomplish great things for the Kingdom.

Barnabas and Saul spent an entire year meeting with "the church"[11] and "taught considerable numbers" (Acts 11:26). It is interesting to note that the number of those being discipled here in verse 26 match the number of those being saved in verse 24: both are said to be "considerable numbers."[12]

The level of discipleship must match the level of evangelism.

Positive response in evangelism calls for discipleship that matches that response, and this was the case in Antioch. The Greek word used for "taught" in Acts 11:26 is the same word used for "teaching" in the Great Commission.[13] The church planters in Antioch were clearly obeying the Lord's command to make disciples and to teach them to obey all that He had commanded them. The Jerusalem church was characterized by "continually devoting themselves to the apostles' teaching" (Acts 2:42), and now the second church plant described in Acts was also spending significant time on discipleship.

The fact that Barnabas and Saul spent an entire year teaching is challenging to church planters today who do not include serious discipleship in their work. Alternatively, the fact that Scripture says that they spent one year and not ten is challenging to other church planters today who focus more on church history instead of Scripture as the norm, and take decades before passing on leadership to local believers. We find in the Antioch church plant a balanced focus on discipleship.

"The disciples were first called Christians in Antioch" (11:26). *Christian* was not a name that the disciples took for themselves. It was what they were called by others.[14] *Disciples*[15] and *believers*[16] are more common words used of followers of Jesus in the book of Acts. An even more common name used by Christians to describe other believers is *brothers*, or *brethren*.[17] To demand that believers refer to themselves as Christians today would seem to be more cultural than biblical. The New Testament uses a variety of words.

Notice the connection between sound discipleship and the new believers being recognized by those around them as Christians. Jesus said, "If you continue in My word, then you are truly disciples of Mine" (John 8:31). It was those who had been discipled in Antioch who were recognized as Christians.

The Direction the Money Flows

> Some prophets came down from Jerusalem to Antioch. One of them named Agabus stood up and began to indicate by the Spirit that there would certainly be a great famine all over

the world. And this took place in the reign of Claudius. And in the proportion that any of the disciples had means, each of them determined to send a contribution for the relief of the brethren living in Judea. And this they did, sending it in charge of Barnabas and Saul to the elders. (Acts 11:27–30)

What we see in this passage is found in many other places in Acts and the New Testament: the church in Antioch collected "a contribution for the relief of the brethren living in Judea." Notice that these verses, which describe the beginning of the church in Antioch, also mention money. It is very significant to note the direction of the money flow in this new church plant. Jerusalem was the mother church. Jerusalem was the established church. Jerusalem was the church with thousands of believers. Antioch was the new church. The new church sends money to the mother church. While this seems interesting to note on this one occasion, it becomes very significant when we realize that this is the consistent pattern[18] found in the New Testament.

_____

In the New Testament money flows away from the new churches, not toward them.

_____

Whenever money is mentioned in connection with a new church in the New Testament, the money flows away from the new church, not toward it. From Acts 18:5 (with 1 Thess. 3:1–2; Phil. 4:16) we can see that money came from new churches in Macedonia to Paul the missionary. Notice that Paul did not send money to the new churches; money flowed away from these churches. Romans 15:26 mentions another offering collected in the newer churches that was sent to the older, more established church in Jerusalem for ministry to the poor in that church. In First Corinthians 16:1–2 Paul gives precise instructions for money to be collected in the newer churches and sent for "the collection for the saints." In Second Corinthians 8:1–5 the generous giving of the churches in Macedonia is again described, this time emphasizing "that in a great ordeal of affliction their abundance of joy and their deep poverty overflowed in the wealth of their liberality" (8:2). If someone might be tempted to discount this pattern because some new church today is economically poor, they should consider that "deep poverty" was the condition of the church in Macedonia. Second Corinthians 11:9 refers to the fact that the brothers from Macedonia supplied Paul's needs. In Philippians 4:15 Paul writes to the Macedonian church in Philippi, thanking them for their generosity and specifically referring to "the first preaching of the gospel." In other words, when they were a new church, they supported Paul.

The use of money is varied in these examples, sometimes going to help the poor in Jerusalem, sometimes going to support missionary work in another city. However, the direction of the money flow remains consistent. In the New Testament money flows away from the new churches, not toward them. This pattern seems consistent with several passages from the Gospels as well (see Matt. 10:9; Mark 6:8; Luke 9:3; 10:4; John 6:27). If the church planter today chooses to follow this example, many problems of dependency in a new church will be avoided before they begin.

The offering collected in the new church in Antioch was to minister to the needs of the poor—believers in new churches are to demonstrate the love of Christ. Jesus had compassion for the sick (see Matt. 14:14; 20:34), the hungry (see 15:32), those mourning the death of loved ones (see Luke 7:12–13), and those who were "distressed and dispirited" (Matt. 9:36). When we consider the direction of the money flow above, the pattern seems to be that sent-out ones focus on evangelism, discipleship and church planting, leaving a local body of believers that then ministers to the poor and needy. Of course, the sent-out ones are to model the Christian life (including ministry to the poor), because they are first followers of Christ and then sent-out ones.

The Multiplication of Churches

> Now there were at Antioch, in the church that was there, prophets and teachers: Barnabas, and Simeon who was called Niger, and Lucius of Cyrene, and Manaen who had been brought up with Herod the tetrarch, and Saul. While they were ministering to the Lord and fasting, the Holy Spirit said, "Set apart for Me Barnabas and Saul for the work to which I have called them." Then, when they had fasted and prayed and laid their hands on them, they sent them away.
>
> So, being sent out by the Holy Spirit, they went down to Seleucia and from there they sailed to Cyprus. (Acts 13:1–4)

The leadership group[19] in the church at Antioch had expanded to include at least five men. As they fasted and prayed one day, the Holy Spirit guided the leaders to release, or send away, Barnabas and Saul for the work to which He had called them.[20] This example suggests that a church that is sensitive to the Holy Spirit, even a church that is relatively new, will be involved in sending out missionaries. As we will see when we discuss Paul's second missionary journey in chapters 7–9 of this book, Paul wrote to the church in Thessalonica months after they had received the gospel and said to them, "The word of the Lord has sounded forth from you, not only in Macedonia and Achaia, but also in every place your faith toward God has gone forth" (1 Thess. 1:8).

The Great Commission was not given only to believers from mature or wealthy churches but to all believers. With the church in Antioch, we begin to see in the book of Acts the *multiplication of churches*. Believers from the Jerusalem church had been scattered and had started the Antioch church, which then sent off missionaries, who would then start multiple churches. Later Paul wrote about this time period and referred to "the churches of Judea" (Gal. 1:22).[21] The Jerusalem church had multiplied into churches in Judea and the surrounding regions.

The Jerusalem church's example highlights the need for churches in the United States and around the world to plant additional new churches locally as well as in distant places. Church planting in new places, where the gospel is not, will extend the breadth of the kingdom of God; church planting where the church already exists will expand the depth of the kingdom of God.[22]

The Jerusalem church's example of multiplication highlights the need for existing churches to plant new churches.

Acts 11 tells us that Barnabas and Saul were the leaders of the Antioch church when it first began to grow. Now in Acts 13 we see five leaders named. Having multiple leaders seems to have prepared the church to release two of their finest without causing concern for the health of the church. The New Testament most often refers to overseers, sometimes called elders or pastors (shepherds), in the plural. As we plant churches, equipping multiple leaders has many positive benefits, one of which is to prepare the church for multiplication. The Holy Spirit's sending out Barnabas and Saul (who would soon be referred to as Paul) was the beginning of Saul's first missionary journey, which resulted in the planting of the next three churches mentioned in the book of Acts.

Overview of the Antioch Church

We found in the Antioch church several common threads that we will see in many of the church plants in the book of Acts. First, the Antioch church clearly demonstrated for us three of the five characteristics of a healthy church noted in Acts 2: discipleship, ministry, and evangelism and missions.[23] Several other common threads were seen here in the Antioch church: the Holy Spirit is the One who saved people, those who believed were discipled, leaders were put in place and the church multiplied.

A unique insight that we gained from the Antioch church, from a principle that we will see repeated, is that money flowed away from the new church. Antioch also provided us with a powerful example of ordinary, nameless Christians bringing the gospel to a place where it had never been, resulting in a new church where there had not been one.

4

THE CHURCH IN PISIDIAN ANTIOCH

Acts 13:13–52

As Barnabas and Paul (as Saul was now called) set out on their missionary journey, they went first to the island of Cyprus,[1] where Barnabas was originally from,[2] and spent some time there. From Cyprus the two sent-out ones sailed to the coast of Asia Minor (modern-day Turkey). It was in this region, in the province of Galatia, that the next three churches in the book of Acts would be planted. In this chapter we will look at the first of these three: the church in Pisidian Antioch.

Challenges to the Church-Planting Team

> Paul and his companions put out to sea from Paphos and came to Perga in Pamphylia; but John left them and returned to Jerusalem. (Acts 13:13)

As the team was setting out from Paphos, on the island of Cyprus, for Asia Minor, team member John Mark left them and returned to Jerusalem. We aren't told why he left, although the wording in Acts 13:13 hints that the leadership of the team may have shifted from Barnabas to Paul,[3] which may or may not have been related to John Mark's leaving the team.

Changes in leadership happen and can be difficult. The church planter should be ready for team members to return home in the middle of a project or for the challenges to relationships that often follow change (see Acts 15:38). It is one of the many trials that a church-planting team may face.

The New Testament provides two important aids concerning unity on teams; these help keep us balanced. First, it clearly alerts us to the reality of challenges. New church planters often naïvely believe that because their work is spiritual and within God's will, they will not experience conflict among team members. God's Word is more in touch with reality than we are. Acts 13:13 clearly describes such challenges.

---

*The New Testament gives clear guidelines to
protect against team challenges.*

Shortly after this first missionary journey to Galatia, Paul wrote back to the churches he had founded in this province and told the believers of the time when he had disagreed with Peter. He was transparent enough to write, "I opposed him to his face" (Gal. 2:11). These same kinds of challenges can face new congregations. After planting the church in Corinth on his second missionary journey, Paul wrote to the church about "quarrels among [its members]" with believers saying, "'I am of Paul,' and 'I of Apollos,' and 'I of Cephas,' and 'I of Christ'" (1 Cor. 1:11–12). Writing to the Ephesian church, which was planted on the third missionary journey, Paul implored the believers to "walk in a manner worthy of the calling with which [they had] been called" (Eph. 4:1). Included in that exhortation to a worthy walk is the instruction to be "diligent to preserve the unity of the Spirit" (4:3). Church planters today should not unduly question their team or church when a challenge to unity develops. Scripture tells us that difficulties will occur.

The second aid that the New Testament gives us to help maintain team unity is a series of clear guidelines on how to protect against the inevitable challenges and how to work through them. We are to be daily filled with the Spirit (see Gal. 5:16; Eph. 5:18), confront serious issues (see Matt. 18:15–17; Gal. 2:11), defer on less serious issues (see Rom. 14:13–14, 19; 15:7) and make forgiveness a normal part of team and church dynamics (see Matt. 18:21–35; Eph. 4:32).

Abundant Gospel Sowing

> But going on from Perga, they arrived at Pisidian Antioch, and on the Sabbath day they went into the synagogue and sat down. After the reading of the Law and the Prophets the synagogue officials sent to them, saying, "Brethren, if you have any word of exhortation for the people, say it." Paul stood up, and motioning with his hand said, "Men of Israel, and you who fear God, listen." (Acts 13:14–16)

We can continue to share the gospel and plant churches wherever we find ourselves, even if the reason we are in a place is due to illness.

Upon the team's arrival in Asia Minor, Paul and his companions traveled overland to Pisidian Antioch, a city in the province of Galatia. According to Galatians 4:13, Paul first came to the Galatian churches "because of a bodily illness."

Sometimes our plans are impacted by unplanned or undesired events. Sent-out ones today should not feel that it is strange for obedient servants of the Lord to become sick (see 2 Tim. 4:20). Notice Paul's example of continuing to share the gospel and plant churches wherever he found himself, even when his reason for being in a specific place was due to illness.

On the Sabbath day Paul and his companions went to the synagogue, as was Paul's custom, and after the Scripture was read, Paul spoke the gospel to the people. It is of note that Scripture was read in the synagogue (see Acts 13:15, 27; 15:21). While other sources tell us many other things about the synagogue of the first century, care is taken here to emphasize a characteristic that the Holy Spirit deliberately included in Scripture. This reading of Scripture prior to the preaching of the gospel is parallel to the broad seed sowing that we saw in the founding of the Jerusalem church: the believers shared publicly about the mighty works of God before Peter preached an evangelistic sermon.[4] It is also parallel to the Ethiopian's reading of Scripture as preparation for hearing the gospel.

Around the world today one strategy of church planters is to make Scripture widely available and to encourage people to read it. Scripture reading or the hearing of Bible stories are good ways for individuals to be prepared for evangelism. Sent-out ones often use the distribution of Bibles, New Testaments, Scripture portions or recorded Bible stories in audio or video formats to prepare the soil of people's hearts for evangelism. "Faith comes by hearing, and hearing by the word of Christ" (Rom. 10:17).

Evangelism with Creation-to-Christ Story

Paul stood up, and motioning with his hand said,

"Men of Israel, and you who fear God, listen: The God of this people Israel chose our fathers and made the people great during their stay in the land of Egypt, and with an uplifted arm He led them out from it. For a period of about forty years He put up with them in the wilderness. When He had destroyed seven nations in the land of Canaan, He distributed their land as an inheritance—all of which took about four hundred and fifty years. After these things He gave them judges until Samuel the prophet. Then they asked for a king, and God gave them Saul the son of Kish, a man of the tribe of Benjamin, for forty years. After He had removed him, He raised up David to be their king, concerning whom He also testified and said, 'I have found David the son of Jesse, a man after My heart, who will do all My will.' From the descendants of this man, according to promise, God has brought to Israel a Savior, Jesus." (Acts 13:16–23)

Paul began his evangelistic presentation in Pisidian Antioch with a story that started in Exodus and moved quickly to the coming of "a Savior, Jesus." Similar stories summarizing the Old Testament, sometimes called creation-to-Christ stories, are found several times in Acts (see 7:2–50; 17:24–31) and are used by church planters today. Sent-out ones combine short (one- to two-minute) overviews of Old Testament stories that combine to provide the overarching story of the Old Testament. Often these individual overviews are later expanded into fuller stories to give a more thorough understanding of the Old Testament.

Paul went from giving an overview of the Old Testament to proclaiming the death, burial and resurrection of Jesus (see Acts 13:29–30), using the Scriptures as his source of authority (see 13:33–35). Notice the similarity of this gospel content to that which Peter proclaims in Acts 2 and 3 and to the definition of the gospel that Paul gives in First Corinthians 15:1–4. The gospel is not just any presentation of good news about God's love but the specific message of the death of Jesus for our sins and of His burial and resurrection according to the Scriptures.

Jesus modeled proclaiming, or heralding, the gospel. When the Lord began His ministry, He proclaimed the gospel (see Matt. 4:23; Mark 1:14). In the middle of His ministry, when He selected the Twelve, we are told that He was proclaiming the gospel (see Matt. 9:35). Near the end of His ministry, Jesus promised that the gospel would be proclaimed in the whole world (see 24:14). Paul too modeled proclaiming the gospel (see Gal. 2:2; 1 Thess. 2:9).[5] As sent-out ones go to the nations today, they, like Jesus and like Paul, are being sent to herald the gospel (see Mark 3:14).

After calling his hearers in Pisidian Antioch to respond with faith and issuing a warning about not accepting, Paul concluded his message.

Guided by the Holy Spirit

The next Sabbath nearly the whole city assembled to hear the word of the Lord. But when the Jews saw the crowds, they were filled with jealousy and began contradicting the things spoken by Paul, and were blaspheming. Paul and Barnabas spoke out boldly and said, "It was necessary that the word of God be spoken to you first; since you repudiate it and judge yourselves unworthy of eternal life, behold, we are turning to the Gentiles. For so the Lord has commanded us, 'I have placed you as a light for the Gentiles, that you may bring salvation to the end of the earth.'"

> When the Gentiles heard this, they began rejoicing and glorifying the word of the Lord; and as many as had been appointed to eternal life believed. And the word of the Lord was being spread through the whole region. (Acts 13:44–49)

When Paul and his team returned the next week, nearly the entire city had assembled to hear the Word of the Lord. The religious leaders, seeing this response, were filled with jealousy and began to contradict Paul's message.

The reality of opposition was clearly seen in the Jerusalem church plant and would continue to be a major issue on Paul's first missionary journey. Sometimes Scripture does not tell us the reason for the opposition, just as church planters today often may not know all the reasons for opposition against them. However, here in Acts the reason is clearly stated: the religious leaders were jealous of the people's response to Paul's message.

Sent-out ones do not go into a spiritual vacuum. When people turn to Christ, they are turning away from their former religion, and the leaders of that religion lose influence, power and authority. Such a loss led to jealousy in Pisidian Antioch.

Paul responded by leaving the synagogue and turning to the Gentiles, having been guided by a passage from Isaiah: "Behold," he told the Jews, "we are turning to the Gentiles. For so the Lord has commanded us, 'I have placed You as a light for the Gentiles, that You may bring salvation to the end of the earth'" (13:46–47).

One common thread that we find woven through the book of Acts is the guidance of the Lord. This first missionary journey had begun because of the Holy Spirit's guidance (see 13:2, 4). Sometimes the Holy Spirit guides us by not allowing us certain options (see 16:6). In Pisidian Antioch His guidance came through God's Word. Paul's quote to the Jews was from Isaiah 49, a passage that is known as the Second Servant Song. In it Isaiah speaks of a "Servant;" in Isaiah's day this might have been understood as referring to the nation of Israel, but in the New Testament we see clearly that the Servant is Jesus.[6] This passage in Acts 13 appears to show Paul applying the Isaiah passage, which was being used by the Holy Spirit to guide Paul in his work.

While workers today need to be careful to not give scriptural authority to a personal application of Scripture that is not a passage's primary teaching, many will find that the Father uses His Word to guide the sent-out one who consistently reads and meditates on the Bible during his or her quiet time. The Holy Spirit provides guidance for the work in this way.

The Gentiles responded to Paul's preaching by glorifying the Word of the Lord, and many of them believed. The Word of God "was being spread through the whole region" (Acts 13:49). We saw this pattern of growth and multiplication in Samaria (see 8:25; 9:31), we saw it with the beginning of the church in Antioch and we will see it in Thessalonica and Ephesus. In the book of Acts, the Word of God and churches often spread together throughout regions.

Person-of-Peace Model

> But the Jews incited the devout women of prominence and the leading men of the city, and instigated a persecution against Paul and Barnabas, and drove them out of their district. But they shook off the dust of their feet in protest against them and went to Iconium. And the disciples were continually filled with joy and with the Holy Spirit. (13:50–52)

The religious leaders continued their opposition and "instigated a persecution against Paul and Barnabas," driving them out of the district. As Paul and Barnabas departed (for the moment) from Pisidian Antioch, they "shook off the dust of their feet in protest."

The Greek verb used for "shook off" is the exact word that the Lord Jesus uses in Matthew 10:14 and Mark 6:11 as He sends out the Twelve and instructs them to look for a person of peace—someone who had been prepared for the gospel and would be receptive to it. As part of those instructions, Jesus tells the disciples to leave any home that would not receive their message, "shaking off" the dust of their feet as they left. This same word is used only two other times in the New Testament: here in Acts 13:51 and in Acts 18:6, when Paul "shook out his garments" and similarly left a group of Jews to go speak to the Gentiles.

Both of the Acts passages seem to be an application of Jesus' command in the Gospels. This appears to give a textual connection between Jesus' instructions to the Twelve and the apostles' actions in the book of Acts.[7]

Go to a new place believing that God is at work and that
He has already prepared some in that place
to receive the message.

It seems that the core of the person-of-peace evangelism model found in Matthew and Mark is for a sent-out one to go to a new place, believing that God is at work and that He has prepared some in that place to receive the message. If the home that he or she enters does not receive the message, the worker is to "shake the dust off" his or her feet and go to the next place, confident that God has prepared people.

Instead of waiting at the first home until its occupants are ready to receive the gospel, the worker trusts that God has already prepared some in that town, and he or she moves on to find those people. This dramatically shortens the timeline of church planting. Like Paul did, many church planters around the world today follow this person-of-peace model as they enter new areas.

As we noted with the church at Jerusalem, opposition and persecution should be considered normal by the church planter. In Pisidian Antioch this opposition did not make the new believers negative. Instead "the disciples were continually filled with joy and with the Holy Spirit" (Acts 13:52).

Leaving does not mean deserting.

Notice that being filled with the Spirit produced the fruit of the Spirit (see Gal. 5:22–23), which includes joy. Jesus had spoken of receiving the Holy Spirit resulting in "rivers of living water" (John 7:38) flowing from a person.[8] In Acts 2:4 we read that the entire church-planting team was filled with the Spirit, and those who responded with faith and repentance to Peter's message were also promised "the gift of the Holy Spirit" (2:38). Now here on Paul's first missionary journey, the disciples are continually filled with joy and the Spirit. When the work of the Holy Spirit through a sent-out one results in transformed individuals who are filled with the Spirit and joy, the gospel becomes contagious, and others are drawn by these transformed lives. This does not mean that all will go smoothly; the opposition only increased as Paul left Pisidian

Antioch. But it does mean that we have victory in the midst of challenging situations.

Paul and Barnabas went from Pisidian Antioch to several towns—Iconium, Lystra and Derbe—and then they returned to Pisidian Antioch. Remember, they had left Pisidian Antioch because they had been driven out of the area (see Acts 13:50). Leaving, however, as we will discuss in chapter 6 of this book, did not mean deserting. It was only a matter of months after they had been driven out that they returned to Pisidian Antioch, encouraging the disciples and establishing leadership in the new church (see 14:21–23; see also the discussion of the establishment of leadership in chapter 5 of this book).

Overview of the Pisidian Antioch Church

In our examination of the church plant in Pisidian Antioch, we once again recognize common threads, and we also gain unique insights. We saw, first of all, that Scripture wisely warns that challenges to team unity will occur, but it also provides clear guidance on how to prevent and resolve this discord.

As Peter had in Jerusalem, the team began the work in this city with people who had been reading Scripture. Paul shared a creation-to-Christ story with a clear presentation of the death of Jesus for sin and of His burial and resurrection according to the Scriptures (which is the gospel that sent-out ones herald). The believers also faced opposition. In the face of that opposition, we gain a unique insight as the Holy Spirit guides Paul through a personal application of Isaiah 49, and the common threads continue as we see the Word of God spread through the whole region. The church-planting team appeared to follow the person-of-peace model in response to opposition, shaking the dust off their feet as they went to the next place—another insight into how we are called to take the gospel to new places. The workers continued to follow the thread: they would return to establish leaders in the church.

But that would not happen until after they started the church in Iconium.

5

THE CHURCH IN ICONIUM

Acts 14:1–23

The team of sent-out ones had been driven out of Pisidian Antioch, but they did not quit and go home. They modeled perseverance in the face of persecution. They went to Iconium, the location of the next church plant in Acts, the second church plant on Paul's first missionary journey.

Developing a Pattern

> In Iconium they entered the synagogue of the Jews together, and spoke in such a manner that a large number of people believed, both of Jews and of Greeks. But the Jews who disbelieved stirred up the minds of the Gentiles and embittered them against the brethren. Therefore they spent a long time there speaking boldly with reliance upon the Lord, who was testifying to the word of His grace, granting that signs and wonders be done by their hands. (Acts 14:1–3)

Paul and Barnabas began by repeating the model they had used in Pisidian Antioch. They went first to those who had been exposed to God's Word in the synagogue and "spoke in such a manner that a large number of people believed, both of Jews and of Greeks."

The sent-out ones "spent a long time there," even though opposition embittered some against them (although eventually they would have to flee for their lives). A pattern is becoming clear. Paul and his team began where the Word of God had been sown. They presented the gospel in such a way that those whom the Spirit had prepared believed. Then they spent time discipling those who believed. Opposition was normal: as in Pisidian Antioch, they were forced to leave momentarily, but they would later return to establish leaders in these new churches in the province of Galatia (see Acts 14:23).

The statement that "a large number of people believed" is reminiscent of the response to the gospel in Jerusalem, where three thousand had believed (see 2:41), and in Antioch, where "a large number" (11:21) had believed. While no number is mentioned regarding Pisidian Antioch, we are told that "the word of the Lord was being spread through the whole region" (13:49).

The word for "number" means "multitude,"[1] and in its several uses here in Acts, it is modified by an adjective meaning "many" or "large."[2] What a wonderful picture of positive response to the gospel.

As we saw in chapter 3 of this book, however, narrative passages such as the ones just mentioned are descriptive in nature, detailing what happened at certain places and times and not stating what will happen in every scenario. These passages do not promise that large numbers will come to Christ every time we share the gospel, but we certainly want to wrestle with the text instead of holding experience (our own or that of others) as the norm. It is easy to look at our personal experience or to read a biography of someone who served a long time with few results and to conclude that little response from people is normal. However, we want to remember that the norm for our faith and practice is God's Word and that no one's experience is to be held at the same level as Scripture.

The Lord testified to His Word, "granting that signs and wonders be done by their hands" (Acts 14:3).[3] No mention is made of signs and wonders in connection with Antioch or Pisidian Antioch. Here in Iconium signs and wonders are mentioned, and in Lystra we are told of a man being healed, but in the three church plants of the second journey (Philippi, Thessalonica and Corinth), no signs, wonders or healings are mentioned.[4] Then in Ephesus, during Paul's third missionary journey, "God was performing extraordinary miracles by the hands of Paul" (19:11).

It appears from the examples clearly described here in Acts 14, as well as one that we see in Acts 3 (the healing of the lame man at the temple), that "signs and wonders" refers to situations in which the sent-out ones were guided to speak to a sick person with whom they came into contact in their daily walk, and whom God then healed (see 3:1–6; 14:8–10). No special healing service is mentioned, nor do the healings appear to be planned activities. These took place in the normal course of daily life. In many parts of the world today, people are coming to faith after God has answered prayers for healing.[5]

Flee to the Next City

> But the people of the city were divided; and some sided with the Jews, and some with the apostles. And when an attempt was made by both the Gentiles and the Jews with their rulers, to mistreat and to stone them, they became aware of it and fled to the cities of Lycaonia, Lystra and Derbe, and the surrounding region; and there they continued to preach the gospel. (14:4–7)

The opposition escalated, reaching a point at which an attempt was actually made to stone the church planters. Paul and his companions became aware of these plans and fled to the next cities, as Jesus had commanded His disciples (see Matt. 10:23).

The Holy Spirit will guide sent-out ones today.

There are times in the book of Acts when believers respond to persecution with prayers for boldness and stay right where they are (see 4:23–31). Other times believers respond by fleeing (see 9:25). Part of the reason for these varying responses may be the difference between persecution that is specific against an individual and persecution that is general against all believers. In Acts 9 the persecution is specifically against Saul, and he responds by fleeing Damascus, whereas in Acts 4 the persecution is general against all believers, and the believers pray for boldness and stay. The Holy Spirit will guide sent-out ones today as to what they should do in each situation.

Fleeing from Iconium did not silence Paul and his team! They "continued to preach the gospel" (14:7) as they went to the next town, Lystra. However, the work in Iconium was not over. Before we look at how the work began in Lystra, we will jump ahead to what happened when the workers returned to Iconium.

Strengthening the Souls of the Disciples

After they had preached the gospel to that city and had made many disciples, they returned to Lystra and to Iconium and to Antioch, strengthening the souls of the disciples, encouraging them to continue in the faith, and saying, "Through many tribulations we must enter the kingdom of God." (Acts 14:21–22)

After preaching the gospel in Lystra and Derbe, we are told in Acts 14:21 that Paul and Barnabas "returned to Lystra and to Iconium and to Antioch."[6] As they returned to these cities, they strengthened the souls of the disciples. We saw earlier that discipleship was emphasized in the first two church plants (see 2:42; 11:26), and now in these next three churches, strengthening the disciples is clearly mentioned.

The sent-out ones specifically strengthened the new believers with encouragement "to continue in *the faith*" (14:22). The same phrase "the faith" is used in Acts 6:7: "A great many of the priests were becoming obedient to *the faith*." When Paul wrote letters a few months after his first journey to these churches, he described his own conversion this way: "He who once persecuted us is now preaching *the faith*." (Gal. 1:23). This wording brings to mind Jude 3, which exhorts believers to "contend earnestly for *the faith* which was once for all handed down to the saints." Perhaps Paul was exhorting the disciples in these three churches to continue in the teaching they had been given, to continue in the faith as they received it.

Discipleship includes sound doctrinal teaching. It is quite interesting to note in Paul's letter to these Galatian churches that soon after Paul's departure others tried to turn the churches against Paul and *the faith*: "They eagerly seek you, not commendably, but they wish to shut you out so that you will seek them" (Gal. 4:17). And some in the Galatian churches were being swayed: "I am amazed that you are so quickly deserting Him who called you by the grace of Christ, for a different gospel; which is really not another;

only there are some who are disturbing you and want to distort the gospel of Christ" (Gal. 1:6–7). Church planters today need to be prepared for the reality that new churches can be attacked by people who want to turn the believers away from sound teaching, away from *the faith*.

Church planters must warn new churches of opposition
and prepare them to withstand attacks.

While it is not pleasant to think about such negative possibilities, the wise church planter recognizes that the New Testament clearly teaches that false teachers will come (see 2 Pet. 2:1) and therefore prepares new churches "to continue in the faith" (Acts 14:22). Here, at the end of his first journey, Paul encourages the new believers to do exactly that. At the end of his third journey, he is even more blunt to another young church: "I know that after my departure savage wolves will come in among you, not sparing the flock; and from among your own selves men will arise, speaking perverse things, to draw away the disciples after them" (20:29–30). Church planters are to warn new churches and prepare them to withstand such attacks.

Paul also encouraged new believers in the new churches to continue in the faith in the face of challenges, saying, "Through many tribulations we must enter the kingdom of God" (14:22). Jesus, Peter and Paul all warned believers of the reality that trials and tribulations would come (see John 16:33; 1 Pet. 4:12; 2 Tim. 3:12). The good news is that God, who is inside every believer, provides us victory in the midst of these difficulties (see John 16:33; Rom. 8:37–39; 1 John

4:4). Sent-out ones must prepare new churches to anticipate
trials and teach them that they can walk victoriously through
these trials by the power of God.

---

*Paul modeled the kind of perseverance through trials that
he encouraged new believers to practice.*

It is interesting to note that these new churches Paul was
speaking to about tribulations were in towns where he was
driven out (Pisidian Antioch), faced attempted stoning (Iconium) and was stoned and left for dead (Lystra). Paul was not
speaking empty words. He modeled the kind of perseverance
through trials that he encouraged the new believers to practice.

Leadership in New Churches

When they had appointed elders for them in every church,
having prayed with fasting, they commended them to the
Lord in whom they had believed. (Acts 14:23)

As Paul and Barnabas returned to Pisidian Antioch,
Iconium, and Lystra, strengthening the disciples, encouraging them to continue in the faith and preparing them for
tribulations, they also "appointed elders for them in every
church."

The church planter is responsible to put leaders in place
in new churches. The leaders here in Acts 14:23 are called elders.[7] In Acts 20 Paul called for the elders of the church in
Ephesus (see 20:17) and told them that the Holy Spirit had
made them "overseers."[8] He instructed these men to pastor, or

"shepherd,"[9] the church (see 20:28). As we saw in chapter 2, this use of these three words—*elders, overseers* and *pastors* (or *shepherds*)—in an interchangeable way is consistent with other passages in the New Testament (see Phil. 1:1; Titus 1:5, 7; 1 Pet. 5:1–2).[10]

In Acts 6 we read that the church was instructed to select the servant leaders "from among [them]" (6:3). We see again in Acts 14:23 that the elders appear to have come from within the churches.[11] Church planters need to look for men in the churches whom the Holy Spirit has gifted as pastor-teachers and who meet the biblical qualifications for leadership (see 1 Tim. 3:1–7; Titus 1:5–9). Having sound leaders in place who can equip "the saints for the work of service" (Eph. 4:12) and build up the church so that the disciples are not spiritually immature, susceptible to "every wind of doctrine" (4:14) will prepare the new churches to withstand the false teachers who will come. Paul appointed the leaders in Pisidian Antioch, Iconium and Lystra with prayer and fasting (see Acts 14:23), which reminds us of how his first missionary journey had begun (see 13:2).

New groups of believers are called churches.

In Acts 14:23 the new groups of believers are called churches.[12] In Jerusalem the group was called a church early on (see Acts 5:11), and the same was true in Antioch (see 11:26). Now these three groups are called churches as well. Later, while on his second missionary journey, Paul writes the new believers in Thessalonica shortly after leaving them and calls them "the church of the Thessalonians" (1 Thess. 1:1).

Missions tradition has sometimes referred to groups of new believers, at least until the group is established, by names other than *church*. It is true that before calling groups *churches*, church planters should take care that the new believers actually practice what the New Testament says about a church.[13] However, the normal New Testament word to describe these new groups is *church*.

Overview of the Iconium Church

We noted that Paul's pattern for evangelism began to emerge in Iconium. It highlights the common threads we have been observing: He and his team began where God's Word had already been sown. They presented the gospel, and some who heard it believed. The apostles spent time discipling the new believers, and they persevered through opposition. They departed the city and they later returned to equip leaders from the new congregation.

We also noted several unique insights. In these cities a large multitude believed. The Holy Spirit guided Paul and his companions in a situation of persecution as to whether they should remain or flee. The workers fled to Lystra and then returned to strengthen the disciples. Discipleship included giving the believers sound doctrinal teaching, which prepares new churches for resisting those who will come in and try to lead them away from sound doctrine and the faith they have received. Paul taught the new believers to persevere while modeling the perseverance he taught.

While we have discussed how the gospel arrived in Pisidian Antioch and Iconium and how these two churches were planted and had leadership put in place, we have not yet examined the planting of the church at Lystra. Now we return to the sequence of Paul's first missionary journey to study how the gospel came to this fifth church.

discipleship is much more than teaching others, but it is showing others how to walk out their faith, no matter what they faceed.

6

THE CHURCH IN LYSTRA

Acts 14:8–28

After reaching Asia Minor on his first missionary journey, Paul went first to Pisidian Antioch, from which he was driven out. He went next to Iconium, where he was stoned and left for dead. Recovering from the stoning, he fled the city. Opposition was present in every city and intensified as the journey progressed.

Now Paul arrived at Lystra.

Altering the Plan

When Paul arrived at Lystra, he deviated from the pattern we have begun to see emerge: he did not begin in a synagogue. Paul would return to his pattern of beginning in the synagogue during his second and third journeys (see Acts 17:2, 10, 17; 18:4; 19:8), but in Lystra no mention is made of the synagogue.[1]

The church planter's goal is to be led by the Spirit and to be willing to depart from his or her plan.

The church planter today may have typical patterns or a plan in mind, but he or she should always remember that the goal is to be led by the Holy Spirit, and be willing to depart from the pattern or plan.

Meeting a Physical Need

> At Lystra a man was sitting who had no strength in his feet, lame from his mother's womb, who had never walked. This man was listening to Paul as he spoke, who, when he had fixed his gaze on him and had seen that he had faith to be made well, said with a loud voice, "Stand upright on your feet." And he leaped up and began to walk. (Acts 14:8–10)

The work in Lystra began with meeting a physical need. Paul observed that a lame man, who had been listening intently to Paul's preaching, had faith to be made well.[2] Paul commanded him to stand up, and the man "leaped up and began to walk."[3]

When Jesus sent out the seventy and instructed them to use the person-of-peace model, He instructed them to "heal those . . . who are sick" (Luke 10:9). As we saw in connection to the work in Iconium, prayer for the sick is normal around the world today. Besides prayer, sent-out ones meet people's physical needs in many other ways as well: running medical clinics, ministering to those suffering from AIDS and drilling water wells, to name a few.

The Challenge of Language

> When the crowds saw what Paul had done, they raised their voice, saying in the Lycaonian language, "The gods have become like men and have come down to us." And they began calling Barnabas, Zeus, and Paul, Hermes, because he was the chief speaker. The priest of Zeus, whose temple was just outside the city, brought oxen and garlands to the gates,

and wanted to offer sacrifice with the crowds. But when the apostles Barnabas and Paul heard of it, they tore their robes and rushed out into the crowd, crying out. (Acts 14:11–14)

The reaction of the people in Lystra to the healing of the lame man did not unfold in a positive way. Instead of giving glory to God for this amazing miracle and desiring to hear more about Him, the people responded by attempting to glorify Paul and Barnabas, saying, "The gods have become like men and have come down to us." They began to call the apostles Zeus and Hermes, names of two of their gods, and the priest of Zeus brought oxen in order to offer Paul and Barnabas a sacrifice.

In verse 14 we are told, "*When* the apostles Barnabas and Paul heard of it, they tore their robes." This indicates an apparent delay between the words of verses 11 and 12 (when the people called the apostles gods), the actions of verse 13 (the priests bringing oxen to sacrifice) and the reaction of Paul and Barnabas in verse 14. The text may indicate the reason for this delay in telling us that the crowds were speaking in the Lycaonian language. This seems to suggest that the language used is significant in understanding what follows. The delay in the sent-out ones' response makes sense if they did not speak the Lycaonian language.

Language certainly can be a barrier in church planting. In Acts 2 the crowd notes that they heard the apostles "in [their] own languages[4] to which [they] were born" (Acts 2:8). On the day the Jerusalem church was born, the gospel was heard in the listeners' mother tongue. This is always the language in which it is best for people to hear the gospel. Later in Acts we find Paul using the trade language, Greek, to speak to a Roman soldier (see 21:37) and then proceeding to speak to the local crowd in Aramaic or the Hebrew dialect, the people's heart language (see 22:2). This caused the crowd to grow quiet and listen more closely. Language can be a barrier to understanding what is going on around us (as in the case we are considering in Lystra) and also to being understood by others.

While Acts 14 seems to indicate that language was a challenge in Lystra, keep in mind (as we will see shortly) that a church was started here (see 14:21, 23)! This challenge of language made the task more difficult, but Paul and Barnabas found a way to share the good news (presumably by working with those who knew Greek), make disciples and plant a church.

Sent-Out Ones

> When the apostles Barnabas and Paul heard of it, they tore their robes and rushed out into the crowd, crying out. (14:14)

Before returning to the flow of the story, let's consider a word used in Acts 14:14, *apostles*, and see how it is applied. The phrase "the apostles Barnabas and Paul" clearly uses the word *apostle* to refer to Barnabas as well as to Paul. The English word *apostles* is a transliteration of the Greek word *apostoloi* (ἀπόστολοι); this means that the translators simply copied the letters of the word into English instead of translating the word's meaning. So what does *apostle* actually mean?

The noun comes from the verb meaning "to send away" or "to send out," hence the term "sent-out ones" or sometimes simply "messengers." The Latin noun *missionarius* comes from the verb *missio*, which means "sending away"; this is how the word *missionary* came into the English language between 1635 and 1645. Thus the English word *missionary* and the Greek word *apostoloi* have the same meaning: one sent out, or sent-out one.

The word is found in the New Testament some seventy-eight times, and in forty-seven of those uses it appears to refer to the twelve apostles.[5] These twelve specific individuals are listed by name on four different occasions.[6] They belong to a definitive group that continues to be recognized as a group in heaven.[7] So today, even if a church planter sent to an unreached people group is named John or Peter, he is not one of the twelve apostles. I like to refer to the original Twelve as "capital-A Apostles." That group has a unique place in salvation history, and no one else will ever join it.

The New Testament uses the word "apostle" to refer to others outside the group of the twelve apostles.

That being said, Acts 14:14 makes it clear that the New Testament does use the word *apostle* to refer to others who are not in this unique group. In Galatians 1:19, James, the half-brother of Jesus, is called an apostle, although he was definitely not one of the Twelve. Adronicus and Junias are included "among the apostles" in Romans 16:7, although they are not among the named Twelve. This broader use of the word *apostle* leaves open the possibility that apostles did not disappear when the last of the Twelve died.

The office of apostle may be a gift given by the Holy Spirit to some in the body of Christ. When First Corinthians 12 and Ephesians 4 mention apostles, the term may apply to gifted men and women in the church beyond the Twelve. It is interesting to note, however, that neither the noun nor the verb form for *apostle* is applied to all Christians in the New Testament. This would be consistent with the implied response to the rhetorical question in First Corinthians 12:29, "All are not apostles, are they?"

The Great Commission was given to all believers.

The Great Commission was given to all believers, and therefore every Christian is to focus on making disciples of all ethnicities as he or she goes through life.[8] But not every Christian is commanded to move to other countries or other people groups to plant churches, as an apostle is. It is not inconsistent with Scripture for some Christians to live in the country in which they were born and to focus on making disciples of every group they come in contact with at home, while perhaps taking advantage of opportunities to go on short-term mission trips.[9]

However, some in the body of Christ are gifted to be "sent-out ones." Paul, who is called an apostle, a sent-out one, more than anyone else in the New Testament, describes the passion of sent-out ones in Romans 15:20–21: "I aspired [made it my goal] to preach the gospel, not where Christ was already named, so that I would not build on another man's foundation; but as it is written, 'They who had no news of Him shall see, and they who have not heard shall understand.'" Sent-out ones go where the gospel is not—where people have never heard or understood who Jesus is. When the sent-out ones get there, they do what the book of Acts pictures them doing: they evangelize and make disciples, leaving behind New Testament churches.

While the New Testament church's job of evangelism is not complete if one lost person in one hundred remains (see Luke

15), sent-out ones are never pictured as staying in one place for long. They go where the gospel is not, they evangelize and make disciples and they build a New Testament church. Then they go on to where the gospel is not, where people have never heard the name of Jesus. The wording of Acts 14:14 clearly expands the meaning of the word *apostle* beyond the Twelve.

Sent-out ones go where the gospel is not; then they evange-lize and make disciples, leaving behind New Testament churches.

Scriptural Authority

When the apostles Barnabas and Paul heard of it, they tore their robes and rushed out into the crowd, crying out and saying, "Men, why are you doing these things? We are also men of the same nature as you, and preach the gospel to you that you should turn from these vain things to a living God, who made the heaven and the earth and the sea and all that is in them. In the generations gone by He permitted all the nations to go their own ways; and yet He did not leave Himself without witness, in that He did good and gave you rains from heaven and fruitful seasons, satisfying your hearts with food and gladness." Even saying these things, with difficulty they restrained the crowds from offering sacrifice to them. (Acts 14:14–18)

"When the apostles Barnabas and Paul heard" of the plans of those in Lystra to offer sacrifices to them because of the healing of the lame man, they did not allow the people to carry out their intentions. Paul and Barnabas made it very clear that they were not superior to their hearers but were men of the same nature as the people, and they had come to preach the gospel. That message was that the people should turn from vain things and turn to God. Instead of worshiping man, they should worship the living God who made "the heaven and the earth and the sea and all that is in them."[10]

Paul quoted from the Scriptures without necessarily referring to the quote as Scripture.

Although speaking to Gentiles who did not have a background in the Old Testament, Paul still quoted from the Scriptures without referring to the quote as Scripture. This provides a good example for church planters today to use Scripture when possible, even if the hearers may not recognize it as such. In doing this, workers model scriptural authority in a way that they can explain after people come to faith.

It is noteworthy that the apostle Paul "restrained the crowds from offering sacrifice" to him (14:18). This is consistent with the apostle Peter not allowing people to bow down to him in Acts 10:26 and the angel in Revelation 22:9 not allowing John to bow down to him, saying, "Do not do that. . . . Worship God." This is an important insight in places where people bow down before figures of these very apostles and other disciples, worshiping the saints.

More broadly, people in many places around the world honor missionaries. While gratitude toward those who bring the gospel to a town or people is normal, church planters should take care that the glory goes to God. While it can be very encouraging for a missionary to receive honor, allowing new believers to exalt him or her may end up hindering the new believers' understanding that the workers' adequacy comes from God (see 2 Cor. 3:5; 4:7) and that they themselves are complete in Him alone (see Col. 2:10).

Opposition Intensifies

> But Jews came from Antioch and Iconium, and having won over the crowds, they stoned Paul and dragged him out of the city, supposing him to be dead. But while the disciples stood around him, he got up and entered the city. The next day he went away with Barnabas to Derbe. (Acts 14:19–20)

Paul and Barnabas' rejection of the offered sacrifices quickly turned the emotions of the people of Lystra. They went from wanting to offer sacrifices to stoning Paul until they supposed he was dead. The Jews who had opposed the church-planting team in Antioch and Iconium had come to Lystra, won over the crowd, and instigated the stoning.

Beware of an unbiblical view of suffering.

This description serves as an important lesson for any church planter today who has believed a prosperity gospel that promises nothing bad will happen to one in God's will. Paul's experience is completely consistent with that of the Lord Jesus or Joseph, Job or Daniel. In Acts 12 we read of Peter's miraculous deliverance from prison (see 12:7–10) but only after we have been told of the martyrdom of James (see 12:2). We need not weep for James: he entered heaven that day! But neither should we agree to an unbiblical view of suffering that suggests that we will experience only comfort and ease if we are obeying God.

Many years after this stoning event, Paul would look back at the "persecutions, and sufferings . . . at Antioch, at Iconium and at Lystra" and testify, "Out of them all the Lord rescued me!" (2 Tim. 3:11). Exactly how the Lord rescued Paul is not clear in Acts 14; the wording allows for the possibility of a miraculous healing but does not explicitly say how Paul was restored after being stoned (see 14:20).

After his stoning Paul went from Lystra to neighboring Derbe before returning to Lystra and also to Iconium and Pisidian Antioch to establish leaders in the new churches in each place.

Leaving Did Not Mean Deserting

> After they had preached the gospel to that city and had made many disciples, they returned to Lystra and to Iconium and to Antioch, strengthening the souls of the disciples, encouraging them to continue in the faith, and saying, "Through many tribulations we must enter the kingdom of God." When they had appointed elders for them in every church, having prayed with fasting, they commended them to the Lord in whom they had believed.
>
> They passed through Pisidia and came into Pamphylia. When they had spoken the word in Perga, they went down to Attalia. From there they sailed to Antioch, from which they had been commended to the grace of God for the work that they had accomplished. When they had arrived and gathered the church together, they began to report all things that God had done with them and how He had opened a door of faith to the Gentiles. And they spent a long time with the disciples. (Acts 14:21–28)

Paul and Barnabas were nearing the end of the first missionary journey. Before going back home, they returned to

Lystra, Iconium and Pisidian Antioch to "strengthen the souls of the disciples, encouraging them to continue in the faith."

In the book of Acts, we read that Paul never stayed more than three years in one place.[11] He stayed as little as three weeks in Thessalonica, as he was forced to leave after persecution (see 17:2–10). However, it was his pattern to return to the new churches,[12] and he stayed in communication with the new believers, writing letters and sending messengers. For Paul, leaving did not mean abandoning.

Acts 14:23 describes the establishing of leaders in each of the three cities. The new groups of believers in each place were called churches. Earlier the church in Jerusalem had been told to "select from among [them]" (6:3) individuals needed to fill positions for service. It seems that the leaders for these three churches also came from within the congregations. The leaders were called *elders*,[13] perhaps indicating the respect in which they were to be held. This same term is used later in Acts for those who are to exercise oversight[14] and to pastor the churches (see 20:17, 28). As we noted with the churches in Jerusalem and Iconium, in the first century *elders*, *overseers* and *pastors* were all words used to describe the same group of men.

The text also indicates that there was more than one leader in each church. This plurality of leadership made it easier for the churches to send out missionaries. If the church planter today helps congregations name multiple leaders, those churches will be better prepared to begin new congregations.

Leaving these three cities and the three new churches, Paul and Barnabas returned to the church in Antioch from which the Holy Spirit had sent them out. The church gathered, and Paul and Barnabas reported on all "that God had done with them and how He had opened a door of faith to the Gentiles" (Acts 14:27). The first missionary journey was over.

Overview of the Lystra Church

During the first missionary journey, we saw the common threads of Paul's pattern. In two of the three cities, he and Barnabas began where the Word of God had already been sown. They presented the gospel, and some who heard it believed. Paul and Barnabas discipled those who believed. Opposition was normal. The workers left temporarily, but they later returned to strengthen the churches. And they established leaders from the congregations in the new churches. While Paul's pattern has become clear to us, we see that he departed from it when necessary.

We gained several unique insights from this church as well. Not knowing the heart language presented a challenge to the sent-out ones at Lystra, yet they planted a church there. The team faced conflict and illness but persevered and saw fruit. Discipleship prepared the new believers to continue in the faith. Paul modeled the perseverance that he called the churches to demonstrate. He and Barnabas followed the person-of-peace model, and the gospel spread through entire regions.

7

THE CHURCH IN PHILIPPI

Acts 15:36–16:34

Paul and Barnabas had just completed their first missionary journey, leaving churches in Pisidian Antioch, Iconium and Lystra. Following this, as we have seen, they returned to their home church in Antioch and reported all that God had done.

After this Paul and Barnabas went to Jerusalem. This visit was in order to quiet some brothers who had distorted the core gospel (see Acts 14:26–15:30). When they departed from Jerusalem to return to Antioch, they were accompanied by Silas and Judas, who shared an encouraging word from the apostles in Jerusalem with the church in Antioch.

"After some days" Paul talked with Barnabas about returning to the churches of the first journey. He wanted to "see how they [were]" (15:36). The second missionary journey, which would result in three new churches, was about to begin. But before they left, the workers would face some challenges.

Challenges to Team Unity

After some days Paul said to Barnabas, "Let us return and visit the brethren in every city in which we proclaimed the word of the Lord, and see how they are." Barnabas wanted to take John, called Mark, along with them also. But Paul kept insisting that they should not take him along who had deserted them in Pamphylia and had not gone with them to the work. And there occurred such a sharp disagreement that they separated from one another, and Barnabas took Mark with him and sailed away to Cyprus. (Acts 15:36–39)

Barnabas wanted to take John Mark, his cousin (see Col. 4:10), on this second missionary trip. Paul did not think this was wise in light of the fact that John Mark had deserted them on the first journey. Because of their differences in perspective, "there occurred such a sharp disagreement that they separated from one another."

Strong gifting or personality traits will cause team members to see situations in very different manners.

The description "sharp disagreement" seems shocking, especially when followed by the fact that this disagreement led to the dissolving of the Barnabas and Paul team. It is interesting to note, however, that the text does not state that either Barnabas or Paul sinned. Remember that Barnabas' real name was Joseph; he had only been given the nickname Barnabas, "which translated means Son of Encouragement" (Acts 4:36), because of his strong gift of encouragement.[1] Remember too that Paul is called an apostle more than anyone else in the New Testament and was strongly gifted as a sent-out one.

These two men were both strongly gifted, but in different areas. On church-planting teams today, strong gifting or strong personality traits can sometimes cause team members to see situations in very different manners. These differences can be challenging. In the book of Acts, we see that such differences led to separation.

New Teams, Same Work

> Paul chose Silas and left, being committed by the brethren to the grace of the Lord. And he was traveling through Syria and Cilicia, strengthening the churches. (Acts 15:40–41)

Both Barnabas and Paul chose new team members and continued with their sent-out work. It is not unusual for circumstances to change and for sent-out ones to serve on a variety of team configurations over the years. "Barnabas took Mark with him and sailed away to Cyprus" (15:39), where they had gone first on their first journey.[2] Paul chose Silas, who had accompanied him and Barnabas from Jerusalem, and traveled overland, going north and then west "through Syria and Cilicia, strengthening the churches."

We gather from this statement that the Antioch church, which was located in the province of Syria, had multiplied locally so that there were now multiple churches throughout Syria.[3] In the United States and around the world, the kingdom of God similarly expands as additional churches are planted in a city or area. The insights we can gain from the church planting that takes place in Acts are beneficial for the first church in a city as well as for additional churches in a city or area.

We are told that several years after his conversion, Paul (then called Saul) was sent home to Tarsus (see 9:30) in Cilicia, and from the statement above it would appear that the gospel had multiplied and that there were churches in Cilicia as well as Syria. The use of *churches*, plural, suggests the spread of the gospel and the multiplication of churches.

Notice too, in this statement, Paul's return visits to strengthen the churches that had been started in Syria and Cilicia. In the book of Acts, leaving does not mean deserting or abandoning.

Workers from the Harvest

> Paul came also to Derbe and to Lystra. And a disciple was there, named Timothy, the son of a Jewish woman who was a believer, but his father was a Greek, and he was well spoken of by the brethren who were in Lystra and Iconium. Paul wanted this man to go with him; and he took him and circumcised him because of the Jews who were in those parts, for they all knew that his father was a Greek. Now while they were passing through the cities, they were delivering the decrees which had been decided upon by the apostles and elders who were in Jerusalem, for them to observe. So the churches were being strengthened in the faith, and were increasing in number daily. (Acts 16:1–5)

God may provide some of your closest colleagues—brothers or sisters in the work—from among those who come to Christ in the next place you take the gospel!

After they had passed through Syria and Cilicia and strengthened the churches along their way,[4] Paul and Silas came to Lystra. One of the disciples in Lystra was named Timothy. While the passage does not clearly say so, it appears that Timothy had grown up in a home in which his Jewish mother and grandmother had regularly shared the Old Testament Scriptures with him (see 2 Tim. 3:15) and that they had come to faith before him (see 2 Tim. 1:5). It seems too that Paul had led Timothy to faith in Christ during his first missionary journey (see 1:2). Now Paul wanted Timothy to join his team.

Notice how this illustrates the saying "Laborers are in the harvest." Timothy was part of the harvest of Paul's first missionary journey, and he would eventually become Paul's most valuable co-laborer. Timothy ended up accompanying Paul on his second and third journeys (see Acts 17:14; 18:5; 19:22; 20:4) and supporting Paul during his Roman imprisonment (see Phil. 1:1; Col. 1:1). In his final letter, which was to Timothy, Paul wrote that he wanted to see him, and he said to him, "Make every effort to come before winter" (2 Tim. 4:21). God may provide some of our closest colleagues—brothers or sisters in the work—from those who come to Christ in the next place we take the gospel!

Now the team consisted of Paul, Silas and Timothy. They returned to the cities in which churches had been planted on the first journey, strengthening the churches. Acts 16:5 says that the churches "were increasing in number daily." It may be that the number of believers in each church was increasing, but the more natural reading of this verse seems to say that the number of churches was increasing. God's Word describes churches that are increasing in number.

Closed Doors

> They passed through the Phrygian and Galatian region, having been forbidden by the Holy Spirit to speak the word in Asia; and after they came to Mysia, they were trying to go into Bithynia, and the Spirit of Jesus did not permit them; and passing by Mysia, they came down to Troas. (Acts 16:6–8)

This passage provides interesting insight into God's guidance for the sent-out task. As the church planters passed through the Galatian region, visiting Lystra, Iconium and Pisidian Antioch, they wanted to go west from that area to Ephesus on the Aegean Sea in Asia. But they were "forbidden by the Holy Spirit." So they started north to Mysia, trying to go further north to Bithynia on the coast of the Black Sea, but the "Spirit of Jesus did not permit them."

Paul encountered closed doors and the breakup of his plans.

While the text does not say how the Holy Spirit stopped them from going to Ephesus or Bithynia, it is clear that Paul experienced closed doors and plans that did not materialize. Later in Acts we see an instance in which the Holy Spirit guided His servant through other believers (see 21:11–14). In chapter 4 of this book we saw that illness can impact a team's plans and influence where the workers go (see Gal. 4:13). However they come about, closed doors can be discouraging to sent-out ones.

This passage makes it clear that even the apostle Paul experienced closed doors. This reminds us that facing a closed door does not necessarily mean that we are out of God's will. Neither does it necessarily mean that we will never do those things we had planned: Paul does get to Ephesus on his third missionary journey (see Acts 19:1). Sometimes closed doors simply mean "not now." Sometimes they just mean that we need to patiently, consistently obey what we already know until God clearly guides us to the next step.

And God clearly guided Paul, Silas and Timothy.

Preach the Gospel

> A vision appeared to Paul in the night: a man of Macedonia
> was standing and appealing to him, and saying, "Come over
> to Macedonia and help us." When he had seen the vision,
> immediately we sought to go into Macedonia, concluding
> that God had called us to preach the gospel to them. (Acts
> 16:9–10)

The missionary team had reached Troas when Paul had a
vision in the night: "A man of Macedonia was standing and
appealing to him, saying, 'Come over to Macedonia and help
us.'" This was the original Macedonian call![5] Paul had wanted
to stay in Asia Minor, to stay closer to home, to stay where
he had already been. But God was calling him to an entirely
new continent: this was a call to Europe. In Troas Luke joined
the team of sent-out ones,[6] and they immediately attempted
to obey the vision, recognizing that God was calling them to
preach the gospel in Macedonia.

---

*Closed doors made it unclear as to where the apostles were
to go, but there was never any doubt as to what they
should do: they were to preach the gospel.*

It is interesting to note that the closed doors they had
recently faced had made it unclear as to where they should *go*,
but Paul's team never had any doubt as to what they should
do: "preach the gospel" (16:10). Remember that in the book of
Acts, as we discussed in chapter 4 of this book, sent-out ones
are sent out to preach the gospel. So Paul and his companions
sailed to Philippi, "which [was] a leading city of the district of

Macedonia" (Acts 16:12). It appears that in going to the city of Philippi, Paul would begin what has been called a "leading-city ministry," in which he went to the primary city of an area and preached, made disciples and planted churches in such a way that the gospel would spread and churches would be planted through that area.

Down by the Riverside

> Putting out to sea from Troas, we ran a straight course to Samothrace, and on the day following to Neapolis; and from there to Philippi, which is a leading city of the district of Macedonia, a Roman colony; and we were staying in this city for some days. And on the Sabbath day we went outside the gate to a riverside, where we were supposing that there would be a place of prayer; and we sat down and began speaking to the women who had assembled.
>
> A woman named Lydia, from the city of Thyatira, a seller of purple fabrics, a worshiper of God, was listening; and the Lord opened her heart to respond to the things spoken by Paul. And when she and her household had been baptized, she urged us, saying, "If you have judged me to be faithful to the Lord, come into my house and stay." And she prevailed upon us. (16:11–15)

Having arrived in Philippi, Paul went on the Sabbath day to a place of prayer outside the gate at the riverside. There he began speaking to the women who had gathered. This location calls to mind the groups all over the world that meet for evangelism or worship in parks and yards, under trees and beside lakes or rivers. Many groups have been started "down by the riverside."

When Paul shared the gospel, he found that the Lord was working: the Lord opened the heart of a woman named Lydia.

She was a businesswoman who sold purple fabrics. She was a "worshiper of God."[7]

Lydia responded to the gospel and was baptized, along with her household. We will see shortly that the Philippian jailer's household was also baptized and that he "believed in God with his whole household" (Acts 16:34).

Lydia opened her home to Paul and his team, and they ministered from there. Lydia seems to be a "woman of peace"—her heart had been prepared ahead of time, and she was ready to receive the gospel.

Challenging Situation

It happened that as we were going to the place of prayer, a slave-girl having a spirit of divination met us, who was bringing her masters much profit by fortune-telling. Following after Paul and us, she kept crying out, saying, "These men are bond-servants of the Most High God, who are proclaiming to you the way of salvation." She continued doing this for many days. But Paul was greatly annoyed, and turned and said to the spirit, "I command you in the name of Jesus Christ to come out of her!" And it came out at that very moment.

But when her masters saw that their hope of profit was gone, they seized Paul and Silas and dragged them into the market place before the authorities, and when they had brought them to the chief magistrates, they said, "These men are throwing our city into confusion, being Jews, and are proclaiming customs which it is not lawful for us to accept or to observe, being Romans."

The crowd rose up together against them, and the chief magistrates tore their robes off them and proceeded to order them to be beaten with rods. When they had struck them with many blows, they threw them into prison, commanding the jailer to guard them securely; and he, having received such a command, threw them into the inner prison and fastened their feet in the stocks.

But about midnight Paul and Silas were praying and singing hymns of praise to God, and the prisoners were listening to them; and suddenly there came a great earthquake, so that the foundations of the prison house were shaken; and immediately all the doors were opened and everyone's chains were unfastened. (Acts 16:16–26)

While going back and forth to the place of prayer, Paul and Silas and the others came across a demon-possessed slave girl who kept crying out when they went past. Paul commanded the demon to come out of her in the name of Jesus. Instead of making everyone happy, this made her owners angry—they were more concerned about making a profit than about the welfare of the girl. They had Paul beaten with rods and thrown in prison.

Church planters have the wonderful opportunity and challenging responsibility of modeling the Christian life for the new believers in the churches being planted.

What Paul and Silas did in prison is extremely important: "About midnight Paul and Silas were praying and singing hymns of praise to God, and the prisoners were listening to them." Paul would later write to the believers in Philippi to "rejoice in the Lord always" (Phil. 4:4), but as we have seen, before Paul admonished others to practice something, he modeled it in his own life. The word *rejoice* is found nine times in the four chapters written to the Philippians,[8] which is interesting because rejoicing appears to have been woven into the DNA of this new church. Church planters have the wonderful opportunity and challenging responsibility of modeling the Christian life for new churches being planted.

God responded to Paul and Silas' prayers and praise by delivering them from prison by means of an earthquake.

When households of friends and family hear the gospel and receive Christ together, gathering together is easy for them and church planting can happen much more rapidly.

A Household Believed

When the jailer awoke and saw the prison doors opened, he drew his sword and was about to kill himself, supposing that the prisoners had escaped. But Paul cried out with a loud voice, saying, "Do not harm yourself, for we are all here!" And he called for lights and rushed in, and trembling with fear he fell down before Paul and Silas, and after he brought them out, he said, "Sirs, what must I do to be saved?" They said, "Believe in the Lord Jesus, and you will be saved, you and your household." And they spoke the word of the Lord to him together with all who were in his house. And he took them that very hour of the night and washed their wounds, and immediately he was baptized, he and all his household. And he brought them into his house and set food before them, and rejoiced greatly, having believed in God with his whole household. (Acts 16:27–34)

The Philippian jailer was about to take his life when Paul assured him that none of the prisoners had escaped. The jailer rushed into Paul and Silas' cell and asked, "What must I do to be saved?" The two sent-out ones shared the gospel with the man's entire household. The whole household believed, so the whole household was baptized.

We see an emphasis on households in the book of Acts. Instead of sharing the gospel with one isolated person, workers generally shared the gospel with entire households. For sent-out ones today, one of the challenges of church planting is connecting individuals who come to faith with other believers in the area, whom the new believers often do not know. When households of friends and family hear the gospel and receive Christ together, gathering will not be an issue for them, and church planting can happen much more rapidly. Departure from New Testament patterns can hinder the response to the gospel that is pictured in the New Testament.

When the chief magistrates sent to have Paul and Silas released the day after their imprisonment, the church planters used their Roman citizenship to gain a more public release. This allowed them to return to Lydia's house to encourage the brethren before leaving Philippi rather than having to flee the city.

Nothing in this Scripture passage suggests that these two house churches (Lydia's and the Philippian jailer's) were merged, but it seems to picture them continuing to meet separately.

Insights from Paul's Epistle to the Philippians

From Paul's letter to the Philippians and those he wrote to other churches, we learn several further details about the church plant in Philippi. Shortly after Paul left the city, the new church sent money to Paul to support him and his work while he was in Thessalonica: "You yourselves also know, Philippians, that at the first preaching of the gospel, after I left Macedonia, no church shared with me in the matter of giving and receiving but you alone; for even in Thessalonica you sent a gift more than once for my needs" (Phil. 4:15–16). The text specifically refers to the time when the church was new: "at the first preaching of the gospel."

Notice again the direction of the money flow. This new Macedonian church, noted for its poverty (see 2 Cor. 8:1–2), did not receive money from the missionary but gave money for the missionary's work in other places. We are told as well that the Philippian church gave liberally to meet the needs of the poor in another place (see 8:1–4). The money was not used to support another church but to support the poor in another place or to support the gospel being spread. Money, again, flowed away from the new church.

From the letter to the Philippians, we also know that church leaders at Philippi included "overseers and deacons" (1:1). Remember that in the book of Acts the terms *elders*, *overseers* and *shepherds* are used interchangeably (see Acts 20:17, 28). Now we learn of deacons also being put in place in Philippi, as they were in Jerusalem (see 6:1–6).

By these examples from his letters, we are reminded that Paul continued to encourage the new Macedonian churches, not just by returning to see them but also by writing them letters and sending others to encourage them. Later in his second missionary journey, Paul would send Silas and Timothy to see how the new brothers in Macedonia were doing (see 18:5; 1 Thess. 3:1–2, 6). Paul would return to these churches at the end of his third missionary journey (see Acts 20:1, 3, 6) and again years later (see 1 Tim. 1:3), following his first

Roman imprisonment. In the book of Acts, leaving does not mean deserting or abandoning.

The letter to the Philippians also reveals that the five characteristics of a healthy church, originally found in the Jerusalem church, are the norm desired for the church in Philippi. First of all, the letter contains the apostle Paul's teaching, which reveals discipleship taking place. We see too that Paul appears to count on a desire on the part of the Philippian church to please him and follow his teaching (see Phil. 1:27; 2:2).[9] Paul taught the Philippians about the identity of Jesus—that He existed "in the form of God" (2:6) while "being made in the likeness of men" (2:7). This is serious doctrinal teaching!

Paul writes about fellowship: he writes of the Philippians' "participation" in the gospel (1:5), which comes from the same Greek word for "fellowship" that describes the Jerusalem church in Acts 2:42.[10] In the same vein he challenges the church to make his joy complete by "being of the same mind, maintaining the same love, united in spirit, intent on one purpose" (Phil. 2:2).

Paul also describes the church as those "who *worship* in the Spirit of God" (3:3) and encourages them to "rejoice in the Lord always" (4:4). Epaphroditus, one of their members, is noted for his *ministry*, and the church is charged to "not merely look out for [their] own personal interests, but also for the interests of others" (2:4). Finally, the church is noted for their *evangelism and missions* by their participation in Paul's missionary work from "the first preaching of the gospel" (4:15).

The standard for the church remained consistent with the standard already laid down.

Overview of the Philippian Church

As Paul's second missionary journey began, we noted a number of unique insights from the founding of the church in Philippi. We saw that the New Testament describes conflict on church-planting teams, which in this case led to the formation of two teams that both continued in the work. As the journey began, we learned that God provided Timothy, who would become Paul's best colleague, from those who had come to faith on Paul's first journey. This shows us that laborers come from the harvest. We learned that closed doors are not unusual for church-planting teams. After Paul's team faced closed doors, God clearly guided them to Macedonia, and they went there, to Philippi, to preach the gospel. God had prepared a woman there named Lydia, and she believed and was baptized, along with her household. Opposition landed Paul and Silas in prison, where they responded with praise and were powerfully delivered.

From Paul's later epistles we noted that money flowed away from the new church in Philippi for the purpose of ministry to the poor and to support mission work in other places.

We saw the common threads of Paul's typical pattern as well. The church in Philippi had overseers/elders/pastors and deacons. Paul left the church but continued to disciple these new believers by writing letters, sending colleagues and returning to them for brief visits. The Philippian church demonstrated the five characteristics of a healthy church: discipleship, fellowship, worship, ministry, and evangelism and missions.

Paul's missionary team obeyed the Macedonian call and preached the gospel in Philippi. A healthy church was planted, and the team went to Thessalonica, the site of the second church plant on the second missionary journey.

8

THE CHURCH IN THESSALONICA

Acts 17:1–15

The second missionary journey began when Paul and Silas left to visit the churches in Galatia that Paul had previously planted. At Lystra they added Timothy to the team. After trying to go to Asia and facing closed doors, the Spirit guided the team to Macedonia, where a church was planted in the city of Philippi.

Now the team traveled southwest in Macedonia and arrived in Thessalonica.

Paul's Custom

> When they had traveled through Amphipolis and Apollonia, they came to Thessalonica, where there was a synagogue of the Jews. And according to Paul's custom, he went to them, and for three Sabbaths reasoned with them from the Scriptures. (Acts 17:1–2)

After leaving Philippi, Paul and his team arrived at Thessalonica, where they spoke to the Jews in the synagogue. What appeared to be a pattern in the first missionary journey (and what has shown up in this book as a pattern of seven common threads) is stated as the custom here.[1] The larger pattern includes these elements:

- Going where the Word of God had already been sown
- Preaching the gospel on the authority of the Scriptures
- Trusting God to draw some to salvation
- Discipling those who believed
- Persevering through opposition
- Putting leaders in place
- Leaving temporarily as necessary

The pattern from Paul's first journey is seen again here in Thessalonica. Paul had a pattern, or plan.

On the first missionary journey, as we noted, Paul started his church plants in the synagogue twice: in Pisidian Antioch (see Acts 13:14–16) and in Iconium (see 14:1). On his second journey he started new churches by going first to the synagogue four times: here in Thessalonica, then later in Berea, Athens and Corinth (see 17:10; 17:17; 18:4). Paul also started a church plant in the synagogue in Ephesus, the focal city of his third missionary journey (see 18:19).[2]

A plan can be good, but God is our guide.

The fact that Paul had a custom but did not follow it in every situation[3] is significant. It is helpful for church planters today to have a plan in mind—to have a vision for how churches are being started in a region or around the world—but at the same time, it is necessary to remember that the book of Acts does not include one model for church planting. God did not

THE CHURCH IN THESSALONICA

begin every church in the first century in one particular way. He chose to tell us about variations in different places. Today too the church planter must be led more by the Holy Spirit than by his or her plan. A plan can be good, but God is our guide.

Paul's Message

> Paul . . . reasoned with them from the Scriptures, explaining and giving evidence that the Christ had to suffer and rise again from the dead, and saying, "This Jesus whom I am proclaiming to you is the Christ." (Acts 17:2–3)

Notice that Paul began in Thessalonica with a clear basis of authority: he "reasoned with them *from the Scriptures.*" In the Jerusalem church plant, we noted the emphasis on scriptural authority (see 2:16), and that emphasis continues throughout the book of Acts. When Paul writes to the Thessalonians, he emphasizes how they had received the message as from God: "You accepted it not as the word of men, but for what it really is, the word of God" (1 Thess. 2:13). When the authority of a church plant is vested in the messengers rather than in God's Word, the leaders become indispensable, and the work seems to progress more slowly. But in Acts, since the authority is in Scripture, Paul is able to leave the groups of new believers, commending them to God and His Word.[4]

May it be obvious to those who hear us that the center of our message is Jesus: His death, resurrection and lordship.

The message that Paul presented with scriptural authority was the death and resurrection of Jesus (see Acts 17:3), which is the core of the gospel (see 1 Cor. 15:3–4). Until people hear about the death of Jesus Christ for their sins and His resurrection on the third day, they are still waiting on the good news. (It is interesting to note that when Paul speaks in the Jewish synagogue here in Thessalonica, he presents Jesus as the Christ. Later in Acts 17 he speaks to Greeks at Mars Hill in Athens and does not mention the name *Christ* at all. This shows Paul contextualizing the gospel for the various groups he addressed.[5])

Notice also in Paul's message in the synagogue his emphasis on Jesus: "This Jesus whom I am proclaiming to you is the Christ" (17:3). Sent-out ones are sent out to proclaim Jesus, to make much of Jesus. When the Jews in Thessalonica began persecuting Paul and the new believers, they summarized the missionary team's message when they accused them of saying that "there is another king, Jesus" (17:7).[6] May it be obvious to those who hear us today that the center of our message is Jesus: His death, resurrection and lordship.

Mixed Response

> Some of them were persuaded and joined Paul and Silas, along with a large number of the God-fearing Greeks and a number of the leading women. But the Jews, becoming jealous and taking along some wicked men from the market place, formed a mob and set the city in an uproar; and attacking the house of Jason, they were seeking to bring them out to the people. When they did not find them, they began dragging Jason and some brethren before the city authorities, shouting, "These men who have upset the world have come here also; and Jason has welcomed them, and they all act contrary to the decrees of Caesar, saying that there is another king, Jesus." They stirred up the crowd and the city authorities who heard

these things. And when they had received a pledge from Jason and the others, they released them.

The brethren immediately sent Paul and Silas away by night to Berea, and when they arrived, they went into the synagogue of the Jews. (Acts 17:4–10)

The response of the Thessalonians to the message was mixed: some were persuaded and joined the team, while others became jealous and actively opposed the team. The book of Acts clearly pictures this mixed response as normal (see 13:48–50; 14:1–2). Sent-out ones should never be discouraged when some do not believe or when people actively oppose them. God's Word clearly tells us that this will happen.

The positive response came from a large number of Greek God fearers who had been listening to the Scriptures as they were read in the synagogues on the Sabbaths. In this we notice again the value of broad seed sowing, of exposing people to God's Word.

The positive response also included "not a few" leading women. The Holy Spirit, through Luke, has noted women responding along with men on several occasions in the book of Acts (see 1:14; 2:18; 5:14; 8:12). Here the status of the women is noted as well: they were leading women, which calls to mind Lydia in Philippi (see 16:14).

Those who had a negative response to Paul's words took the message of Christ's lordship and distorted it as a political challenge to Caesar (see 17:7). The opposition focused on the local person (Jason) who had facilitated the church-planting team. It is interesting to note in Romans 16:21 that a man named Jason is listed as a fellow worker of Paul's (although we cannot say with certainty that this Jason is the same as the one mentioned in Acts).

In the face of this opposition, the brethren sent Paul and Silas away. This is yet another of the various responses to persecution that we see in the book of Acts. Remember that in Acts 4 we read of broad persecution, and we are not told of anyone fleeing; instead the church prayed for boldness (see 4:29–31). And in Acts 9 we read of persecution that seems to be specifically against Saul in Damascus; he fled, being let down in a basket over the wall (see 9:25). Now here in Thessalonica the brethren send Paul and Silas away by night (see 17:10). Remember that Jesus explicitly taught that a normal response when persecuted in one city is to flee to the next (see Matt. 10:23).

It is wise for workers to listen to local brethren in tense situations. Sometimes the right response to persecution is to flee to the next city. Sometimes the right response is to remain and to pray for boldness. Listening to local brethren is important. Following the Holy Spirit's guidance in each situation, however, is the most important key.

In tense situations it is wise for outsiders to listen to local brethren.

The Bereans

The brethren immediately sent Paul and Silas away by night to Berea, and when they arrived, they went into the synagogue of the Jews. Now these were more noble-minded than those in Thessalonica, for they received the word with great eagerness, examining the Scriptures daily to see whether these things were so. Therefore many of them believed, along with a number of prominent Greek women and men. But when the Jews of Thessalonica found out that the word of God had been proclaimed by Paul in Berea also, they came there as well, agitating and stirring up the crowds. Then immediately the brethren sent Paul out to go as far as the sea; and Silas and Timothy remained there. Now those who escorted Paul brought him as far as Athens; and receiving a command for Silas and Timothy to come to him as soon as possible, they left. (Acts 17:10–15)

When Paul and Silas were sent from Thessalonica to Berea, they went to the synagogue and continued to proclaim the Word. As we noted at the beginning of Paul's second journey, closed doors may impact where a sent-out one *goes*, but what the sent-out one *does* is consistent and clear: sent-out ones are sent to herald the gospel.

The response of the Bereans to the gospel is significant: "They received the word with great eagerness, examining the Scriptures daily to see whether these things were so." The appropriate way for people to appraise any new teaching is to examine that teaching in the light of Scripture. All that is commanded in Scripture must be kept. All that is forbidden in Scripture must be rejected. All that is consistent with Scripture (things not commanded or forbidden) may be either kept or set aside, as is fitting in each situation.

Visiting the churches we have founded, sending others to them and corresponding with them are still excellent ways for church planters to continue investing in new churches.

The opposition to Paul's team in Berea was so intense that the workers were immediately driven away, and we are

not told whether or not a church was begun here.[7] In Berea
the antagonism seems to have been even more narrowly focused than it had been in Thessalonica, and only Paul was
sent away by the brethren, this time to Athens. Silas and
Timothy remained in Berea and then apparently joined
Paul in Athens later.

A short period of time[8] after leaving Thessalonica, Paul
was anxious to see how the new believers were doing (see
1 Thess. 3:1), so he sent Timothy and Silas to check on the
new churches at Thessalonica and Philippi.[9] Notice again that
for Paul, leaving did not mean deserting. While he had been
forced to leave these congregations after only a short period of
time, he did not desert them but kept sending team members
back to check on them. After he heard that they were thriving
(see 3:6–8), Paul also wrote to them to encourage them and
to answer specific questions that they had. Visiting, sending
others and corresponding are still excellent ways for church
planters to continue investing in new churches.

Working Night and Day

> You recall, brethren, our labor and hardship, how working
> night and day so as not to be a burden to any of you, we pro-
> claimed to you the gospel of God. (2:9)

Paul wrote to the Thessalonians shortly after leaving there
(see 2:17), giving us additional insights into this church plant.
While we are told of Paul being in Thessalonica for only several weeks (see Acts 17:2), it was sufficient time for the brethren to notice Paul's hard work.

Hard work was characteristic of Paul. He would later
remind the elders from Ephesus of his nonstop laboring
for them: "Night and day . . . I did not cease to admonish

each one with tears" (Acts 20:31). Jesus taught this same emphasis on work: "We must work the works of Him who sent Me as long as it is day; night is coming when no one can work" (John 9:4). In his closing words to the church at Rome, Paul sends greetings to some friends in the church there and recognizes them for their work: "Greet Tryphaena and Tryphosa, workers in the Lord. Greet Persis the beloved, who has worked hard in the Lord" (Rom. 16:12). Paul worked hard, and church planters today would do well to be hard workers. Paul not only mentioned that he worked hard, he repeated the same references to time: "night and day." Sometimes our work, or our work with certain people, can best be done in the day. Work with other people has to be done at night.

The church planter must be willing to adjust his or her personal preferences to the opportunities that come to evangelize and disciple people, night and day.

Remember Nicodemus, a ruler of the Jews, who "came to Jesus by night" (John 3:2). The text does not tell us why Nicodemus came at night, but it is still true today that some people are more comfortable talking about faith in Jesus when the conversation is less visible to others.[10] This can be true of those who are involved in another religion. Or sometimes a conversation at night provides a seeker some private space to gain more information before he or she decides to follow Jesus. For others nighttime is when long conversations are normal. It is interesting to note how many Muslims come to faith during the wee hours of the morning. The church planter must be willing to adjust his or her personal preferences to the opportunities to evangelize and disciple, both night and day.

The Spirit's Conviction

> For this reason we also constantly thank God that when you received the word of God which you heard from us, you accepted it not as the word of men, but for what it really is, the word of God, which also performs its work in you who believe. (1 Thess. 2:13)

> For our gospel did not come to you in word only, but also in power and in the Holy Spirit and with full conviction; just as you know what kind of men we proved to be among you for your sake. (1:5)

From Paul's letter to the Thessalonians, we learn that the new believers received the gospel message as the Word of God and that because of the Holy Spirit's working, the message was powerful and brought full conviction. This makes all the difference in the work. When the message is boring or disconnected, people's response is normally slow; but when the hearers sense inside themselves that the message is true, their response is very different.

Spiritual growth for new believers involves becoming imitators of those who bring them the good news.

This underscores the need for the church-planting team to be focused on prayer and filled with the Holy Spirit.[11] The sent-out one is responsible to boldly share the gospel (see Eph. 6:19) and to make the message clear (see Col. 4:4). However, it is the Holy Spirit who convicts the world of sin, righteousness and judgment (see John 16:8). Just as the Jerusalem church began with people who were "pierced to the heart" (Acts 2:37) upon hearing the gospel, the Thessalonian church began with people who experienced full conviction by the Holy Spirit.

Imitating and Mentoring

> You also became imitators of us and of the Lord, having received the word in much tribulation with the joy of the Holy Spirit, so that you became an example to all the believers in Macedonia and in Achaia. For the word of the Lord has sounded forth from you, not only in Macedonia and Achaia, but also in every place your faith toward God has gone forth, so that we have no need to say anything. (1 Thess. 1:6–8)

In the letter to the Thessalonians, we learn that spiritual growth for the new believers involved becoming imitators of those who had brought them the good news.[12] Paul encouraged the Corinthian church as well, "Be imitators of me, just as I also am of Christ" (1 Cor. 11:1). And he wrote to the Philippians, "The things you have learned and received and heard and seen in me, practice these things, and the God of peace will be with you" (Phil. 4:9).

For the church planter, modeling the Christian life is indispensable to the sound discipleship of new believers. The sent-out ones cannot simply teach the right things; they must be practicing and modeling those same things in their own lives. Sometimes more is caught than taught—what is observed by new believers is more powerful than what they hear. The Thessalonians received the message as God's Word with full conviction, and they became imitators of Paul, Silas and Timothy.

The Thessalonians then became examples to others, and the Word of the Lord went out from them (see 1 Thess. 1:7–8). Remember that Acts 17:2 specifically mentions a short period of time—three weeks—before persecution drove out the team, and then 1 Thessalonians 2:17 clearly says that the missionary team has been gone "for a short while." Yet in these two short periods of time "the church of the Thessalonians" (1:1) grew in "faith and love" (3:6) and continued to "stand firm in the Lord" (3:8), and from them "the word of the Lord [had] sounded forth" (1:8).

Neither the Samaritan woman nor the delivered demoniac nor the Thessalonians understood everything about the gospel, but what they did know they were able to share with others.

This is like the Samaritan woman who met Jesus and immediately went home and testified about what she had experienced (see John 4:28–29, 39). It is like the demoniac who met Jesus and wanted to accompany Him but was told by Jesus, "Go home to your people and report to them what great things the Lord has done for you" (Mark 5:19). Neither of these new believers understood everything, nor did the Thessalonians, but what they did know they shared with others.

Remember that this insight from the second missionary journey was seen during the first journey, when "the word of the Lord was being spread through the whole region" (Acts 13:49) from Pisidian Antioch. Later we will see it again in the third missionary journey, when the Word spread through Asia from its beginnings in Ephesus (see 19:10). It is interesting to note that during this time Paul was enlisting churches specifically to pray "that the word of the Lord [would] spread rapidly and be glorified" (2 Thess. 3:1). Acts does not tell us that the Word spread like this from every city, but it is mentioned regarding several cities and certainly is not unusual.

Overview of the Thessalonian Church

The five characteristics of a healthy church found in the Jerusalem church and later in the church in Philippi are also present in the church in Thessalonica. Paul's two letters to the Thessalonians were part of Paul's ongoing *discipleship* of the new church. His in-depth teaching on Christ's second coming (see 1 Thess. 4:13–5:3) provided sound doctrinal teaching for the new church and for believers throughout the ages.

The *fellowship* seen in the Thessalonian church was a model for others, then and now: "Now as to the love of the brethren, you have no need for anyone to write to you, for you yourselves are taught by God to love one another; for indeed you do practice it toward all the brethren who are in all Macedonia. But we urge you, brethren, to excel still more" (4:9–10).

Paul's instructions strengthened their *worship*: "Rejoice always; pray without ceasing; in everything give thanks; for this is God's will for you in Christ Jesus. Do not quench the Spirit" (5:16–19).

Paul commended their *ministry*, or service (see 1:3), but he also admonished them to continue to serve (see 2 Thess. 2:16–17; 3:13).

And Paul observed that *evangelism and missions* were part of the church just months after the believers had come to faith: "The word of the Lord has sounded forth from you, not only in Macedonia and Achaia, but also in every place your faith toward God has gone forth, so that we have no need to say anything" (1 Thess. 1:8). The five characteristics found in the Jerusalem church were the standard for the church in Thessalonica.

We saw in the church plant in Thessalonica Paul's usual custom, or plan, for his work: go where the Word of God had been sown, preach the gospel, trust God to draw some to salvation, disciple those who believe, persevere through opposition, leave temporarily as necessary, establish leaders from the new congregation. This plan, however, was not always followed. A plan is good, but God is our guide.

Paul presented the gospel with Scripture as his authority. The message was so clear that those opposing it knew it was about Jesus as king. Opposition came, and the brethren sent Paul and Silas away. Paul continued to disciple and strengthen the new church by sending colleagues, writing letters and returning for short visits.

From his letters to the Thessalonians, we learn that Paul had worked hard among them, night and day. The Holy Spirit brought conviction to the hearers in Thessalonica, and the Thessalonians imitated Paul and then became examples for others to follow. And finally, we noted that the five characteristics of a healthy church—discipleship, fellowship, worship, ministry, and evangelism and missions—were found in the Thessalonian church.

9

THE CHURCH IN CORINTH

Acts 18:1–22

Paul, on his second missionary journey, had already planted the churches in Philippi and Thessalonica. Now he concluded his second journey with the church plant in Corinth.

In Corinth Paul stayed eighteen months—longer than he had in any other place on his first or second journey. As we saw in chapter 3 of this book, where we noted that Paul spent a year in Antioch,[1] eighteen months represents a significant amount of time for Paul to be "teaching the word of God among" (Acts 18:11) new believers. On the other hand, in most examples from missions history, leaving a city after only eighteen months of missionary work would be difficult.

Discipling Faithful People: Aquila and Priscilla

[Paul] left Athens and went to Corinth. And he found a Jew named Aquila, a native of Pontus, having recently come from Italy with his wife Priscilla, because Claudius had commanded all the Jews to leave Rome. He came to them, and because he was of the same trade, he stayed with them and they were working, for by trade they were tent-makers. (18:1–3)

In Second Timothy 2:2 we find a key command of the New Testament regarding spiritual multiplication. In this verse Paul commands Timothy to entrust the things that Paul has taught him "to faithful men who will be able to teach others also." As Paul began his ministry in Corinth, "he found" a couple named Aquila and Priscilla who, like him, were tentmakers by trade, and "he stayed with them." The investment Paul made in this couple was later passed on to others in many places because Aquila and Priscilla were faithful people who were able to teach others also. Let's look at how this unfolded.

Paul "went to Corinth. And he found a Jew named Aquila." The impression we get from this verse is that Paul found this man and his wife, Priscilla, shortly after arriving in the city. Aquila also had just arrived, "having recently come from Italy with his wife Priscilla, because Claudius had commanded all the Jews to leave Rome." So religious or ethnic persecution had forced this couple to leave Rome, and they had recently arrived in Corinth.

When Paul left Corinth eighteen months later, Aquila and Priscilla left with him (see Acts 18:18). We are told that Paul moved his ministry in Corinth from one place to another, but we are not told that he stayed with anyone else in this city.[2] If Paul stayed with this couple for eighteen months, it would appear that he discipled them soundly.

When Aquila and Priscilla left with Paul, they accompanied him as far as Ephesus, where they remained after Paul continued on to Jerusalem (see 18:18–19). In Ephesus Aquila and Priscilla hosted a church that met in their house, which we assume they started. When Paul wrote a letter from Ephesus (see 1 Cor. 16:8) back to the

Corinthians, he sent greetings from Aquila and Priscilla, whom the Corinthians would have remembered: "Aquila and Prisca greet you heartily in the Lord, with the church that is in their house" (16:19).[3] Later Aquila and Priscilla moved back to Rome, where they again hosted a church in their home. When Paul wrote a letter to the Romans, he sent greetings to this couple: "Greet Prisca and Aquila, my fellow workers in Christ Jesus, who for my life risked their own necks, to whom not only do I give thanks, but also all the churches of the Gentiles; also greet the church that is in their house" (Rom. 16:3–5).

Aquila and Priscilla appear to be another example of ordinary Christians, like those in Acts 11, who share the gospel and start churches wherever they go that does not have a church.

While Aquila and Priscilla are never called missionaries or apostles, we see that wherever this couple went for years after being discipled by Paul, they started (or at least hosted) churches in their home. They appear to be another example of ordinary Christians, like those in Acts 11, who share the gospel and start churches wherever they go (see 11:19–21). We are not told how old they were; later in their lives Aquila and Priscilla may have gone to other places and started more churches.

Only eternity will reveal the fruit that results when sent-out ones carefully disciple faithful people who will be able to tell others also.

Tentmaking

> Because he was of the same trade, he stayed with them and
> they were working, for by trade they were tent-makers. And
> he was reasoning in the synagogue every Sabbath and trying
> to persuade Jews and Greeks. But when Silas and Timothy
> came down from Macedonia, Paul began devoting himself
> completely to the word, solemnly testifying to the Jews that
> Jesus was the Christ. (Acts 18:3–5)

We have noted the long-term impact of Paul finding Aquila and Priscilla, his discipling them for eighteen months, and
their passing on what they received to others also. Acts 18 also
mentions that the reason he stayed with them was "because he
was of the same trade"—that of tentmakers. While the topic
of tentmaking has been popular in missions recently, this concept actually finds its origin and its name in Paul planting a
church in Corinth. Upon arriving in this city, Paul spent his
time during the week working as a tentmaker (see 18:3). During these months he dedicated his available time to ministry:
"He was reasoning in the synagogue every Sabbath and trying
to persuade Jews and Greeks." Why did Paul work making
tents during this time? Acts 18:5 provides insight.

One reason for tentmaking is to supply financial support.

But first let's set some context. Remember that Paul arrived in Corinth at the end of his second missionary journey,
having previously planted churches in Philippi and Thessalonica. Shortly after Paul's arrival in Corinth, Silas and
Timothy joined him from Macedonia (where both Philippi

and Thessalonica were). Paul had been forced to leave Thessalonica after preaching only three Sabbath days there (see 17:2). He had eagerly wanted to return to see how the new believers were doing (see 1 Thess. 2:17–18), but being unable to do so, he sent Timothy to the Thessalonians (see 1 Thess. 3:1–2) and apparently sent Silas to the Philippians (see Acts 18:5).

Now, as Timothy and Silas joined Paul in Corinth, they brought with them a generous gift that the Philippians had collected to support Paul's work (see 18:5; Phil. 4:15). So "when Silas and Timothy came down from Macedonia [with this gift], Paul began devoting himself completely to the word" (Acts 18:5). Paul worked during the week as a tentmaker until he received the offering from the Philippians. As soon as he received that economic support, he dedicated himself full time to the ministry. It appears that the reason Paul worked as a tentmaker, and one reason people do so today, was out of economic necessity. He supported his church planting with secular work, using his skill in a trade. One reason for tentmaking is economic need.

Another reason for tentmaking is to provide a worker entrance to a city. We see an example of such a motive in 1 Samuel 16. The Lord had commanded the prophet Samuel to go to Bethlehem and anoint one of the sons of Jesse as the next king. Samuel asked how he could do that since Saul would kill him when he heard of it. The Lord told him, "Take a heifer with you and say, 'I have come to sacrifice to the LORD'" (16:2). Sacrificing a heifer provided Samuel a secondary, legitimate reason to be in the city while he obeyed the Lord's primary command.

The Lord has commanded sent-out ones to go—and sometimes getting a legitimate job is an excellent means of gaining entrance into the place God has sent a worker. Tentmaking provides a legitimate reason to be in a city. Integrity suggests, of course, that sent-out ones should do all they have committed to do concerning their tentmaking job; their work should be legitimate. So the first reason for tentmaking is economic; the second is for an entrance into a city or country.

While Paul was involved in tentmaking, he maintained his focus on the spiritual reason he was in Corinth.

While Paul was involved in tentmaking, he maintained his focus on the spiritual reason he was in Corinth: "He was reasoning in the synagogue every Sabbath and trying to persuade Jews and Greeks" (Acts 18:4). It can be easy for tentmakers to get so caught up in their "day job" that they don't spend the time that is available on spiritual reasons they are in the city. Paul kept the balance. At this point in time he did not have the option of working full time as a church planter, but he made sure that he dedicated all the time he could to the main thing. A great deal can be accomplished when the church planter focuses one full day a week on evangelism, discipleship and church planting.

Also we notice an insight into the balance of tentmaking with church planting. While he worked as a tentmaker, Paul spent as much time as he could on church planting. When his financial situation changed, Paul did not maintain the same emphasis on making tents; he "began devoting himself completely to the word" (Acts 18:5). If the reason for tentmaking is to provide entrance into a city or country, the sent-out one should show integrity in honoring his or her commitments. However, the goal is to spend as much time as possible (within the bounds of integrity) on the more primary task of church planting.

The Direction of the Money Flow

> When Silas and Timothy came down from Macedonia, Paul began devoting himself completely to the word, solemnly testifying to the Jews that Jesus was the Christ. (18:5)

The verses describing the church plant in Corinth provide another clear example of the direction that money flows in the book of Acts. We saw this example in Acts 11:29 with the church in Antioch.[4] The new church in Antioch did not receive money from the older, more established, larger Jerusalem church. Instead, the new church sent an offering to the older church. The motive on that occasion was to give to the needs of the poor. The direction of the money flow was away from the new church.

The motive for the Macedonians' offering was for missionary work—for the extension of the gospel in the next cities where churches would be planted.

Here in Corinth Silas and Timothy joined Paul, bringing with them an offering from the churches of Macedonia. The motive for this offering was for missionary work—for the extension of the gospel in the next cities. Even more remarkable, this new church at Philippi had already provided gifts for missionary work—while Paul was in Thessalonica[5] (see Phil. 4:16)! The Philippian church was known for being poor (see 2 Cor. 8:2) and was very new. Yet the direction of the money flow is quite clear: money flowed away from and not toward the new church. Paul received this gift while here in Corinth.

The Person-of-Peace Model

> When [the Jews in Corinth] resisted and blasphemed, [Paul] shook out his garments and said to them, "Your blood be on your own heads! I am clean. From now on I will go to the Gentiles." Then he left there and went to the house of a man named Titius Justus, a worshiper of God, whose house was next to the synagogue. Crispus, the leader of the synagogue, believed in the Lord with all his household, and many of the Corinthians when they heard were believing and being baptized. (Acts 18:6–8)

After Paul received the offering from Philippi and began dedicating himself full time to the work in Corinth, he found resistance in the synagogue. So Paul left the synagogue and began teaching next door in the house of Titius Justus. The manner in which he left connects this passage to Jesus' command regarding a person of peace (see Matt. 10:14; Mark 6:11).

When the listeners in the synagogue resisted and blasphemed, Paul "shook out his garments" and left the synagogue. This is the fourth and final use in the New Testament of this verb "to shake out."[6] Once again we see that Paul did not respond to these resistant people by building relationships with them and patiently waiting until they responded to the gospel. He shook out his garments and boldly told them that their blood would be on their own heads.[7]

On his first missionary journey, Paul had been working in small towns, in more rural settings. When he shook off the dust in Pisidian Antioch, he went to the next town (see Acts 13:51). In Corinth, however, Paul was in a major city. Shaking the dust off here simply meant that he went next door to the home of Titius Justus, "whose house was next to the synagogue" (18:7). Applying the person-of-peace model in a city would not necessarily mean leaving the city but rather going to another group or location in the city.

It is noteworthy that Paul's bold confrontation of the Jews in leaving the synagogue seems to have had a positive effect; the next verse says that "Crispus, the leader of the synagogue, believed in the Lord with all his household" (18:8). When a sent-out person follows the person-of-peace model and leaves those who resist, it does not mean that the sent-out one does not care about those resisting; it simply reflects the sent-out one's confidence that the best thing any believer can do is follow Jesus' model. The best way for a sent-out one to see resistant people come to faith is to walk in the center of God's will, obeying all His Word.

Paul did not respond to people's resistance by building relationships with them and patiently waiting until they responded to the gospel. He moved on and found a person who was ready to receive the message.

When the sent-out one focuses on those whom the Spirit has prepared, a New Testament church may be established. That new church is made up of individuals whose lives have been changed by salvation and the filling of the Spirit. Those transformed individuals will daily model in their community the difference that Jesus can make in someone's life. They will speak the language and understand the culture better than the church planter did. The best way for resistant people to come to faith is when a New Testament church made up of transformed neighbors shares the gospel and models the love of Christ in their community until Jesus returns.

When the sent-out one follows the person-of-peace model, he or she is not showing indifference to resistant people but providing them the best opportunity to come to faith.

Do Not Be Afraid Any Longer

> The Lord said to Paul in the night by a vision, "Do not be afraid any longer, but go on speaking and do not be silent; for I am with you, and no man will attack you in order to harm you, for I have many people in this city." (Acts 18:9–10)

After leaving the synagogue and moving his ministry to the home of Titius Justus, "Crispus, the leader of the synagogue, believed in the Lord with all his household," and "many of the Corinthians when they heard were believing and being baptized" (18:8). In the midst of this powerful work of God, the Lord spoke to Paul in a vision one night. His words are not what we would expect. Everything seemed to be going well, not to mention that this was the great apostle Paul, yet the Lord said to him, "Do not be afraid any longer." Paul was commanded to stop an activity in which he had been engaged—being afraid. We often think of Paul's success and put him in a near superhuman category. The Lord's words to Paul show us that he was more like us than not.

When Paul wrote to the church in Corinth a couple years after this,[8] he reflected on the internal struggles he'd had when he first brought the gospel to them. He wrote, "When I came to you . . . I was with you in weakness and in fear and in much trembling" (1 Cor. 2:1, 3). The words in his letter match the words of the Lord in the vision.

Paul really had been afraid. He really had been "in fear and in much trembling." Remember that Corinth was the last stop on Paul's second missionary journey. In the first city on this journey, Philippi, Paul had been beaten and thrown into prison (see Acts 16:23). He had been run out of the second city, Thessalonica, after only a few weeks there (see 17:2, 10), and shortly after that he had been run out of Berea (see 17:13–14). And he had been mocked in Athens (see 17:32). Then he had come to Corinth. During his first missionary journey, as well, Paul had experienced increasing persecution that had eventually led to his being stoned and left for dead (see 14:19). It is no wonder that he was confronted by fear!

God can use people who become afraid in the sent-out task.

Of course, the Lord's command was that Paul not continue in that fear, because the Lord was with him (see 18:9–10). We too are told not to be afraid, just as Paul was.[9] We can take courage in the knowledge that God can use people who get afraid in the church planting task, in the sent-out task. When we put the people whom God used in the New Testament in a separate category from us and assume that God cannot use us as He used them, we misunderstand Scripture. When James writes about an Old Testament hero, he mentions that he "was a man with a nature like ours" (James 5:17).

The Holy Spirit is the One who worked through these people, and He is the One who lives in us. Paul wrote, "We have this treasure in jars of clay" (2 Cor. 4:7, ESV). The power for Paul to take the gospel to people came from the Holy Spirit (see Acts 1:8), not from Paul being superhuman. The church in Corinth was planted by a sent-out one who struggled with being afraid, and God uses people just like that to plant churches today.

Teaching the Word of God

He settled there a year and six months, teaching the word of God among them.

But while Gallio was proconsul of Achaia, the Jews with one accord rose up against Paul and brought him before the judgment seat, saying, "This man persuades men to worship God contrary to the law." But when Paul was about to open his mouth, Gallio said to the Jews, "If it were a matter of wrong or of vicious crime, O Jews, it would be reasonable for me to put up with you; but if there are questions about words and names and your own law, look after it yourselves; I am unwilling to be a judge of these matters." And he drove them away from the judgment seat. And they all took hold of Sosthenes, the leader of the synagogue, and began beating him in front of the judgment seat. But Gallio was not concerned about any of these things.

Paul, having remained many days longer, took leave of the brethren and put out to sea for Syria, and with him were Priscilla and Aquila. In Cenchrea he had his hair cut, for he was keeping a vow. They came to Ephesus, and he left them there. Now he himself entered the synagogue and reasoned with the Jews. When they asked him to stay for a longer time, he did not consent, but taking leave of them and saying, "I will return to you again if God wills," he set sail from Ephesus.

When he had landed at Caesarea, he went up and greeted the church, and went down to Antioch. (Acts 18:11–22)

While the book of Acts pictures the gospel spreading, it also clearly emphasizes sound discipleship.

Paul was encouraged by the vision from the Lord and settled down in Corinth for his longest season of ministry up to this point in the book of Acts. It is important that we notice how Paul spent his eighteen months in Corinth: "He settled there a year and six months, teaching the word of God among them."

We have noticed a strong emphasis on discipleship in several of the churches in Acts. In Jerusalem the believers "were continually devoting themselves to the apostles' teaching" (2:42). In Antioch, the next church plant, Barnabas and Saul met with the church for an entire year "and taught considerable numbers" (11:26). Paul returned to the church plants from his first missionary journey at the end of the journey, "strengthening the souls of the disciples" (14:22). He also came back to those same churches as he began the second missionary journey, again "strengthening the churches" (15:41). And Paul settled down in Corinth for eighteen months "teaching the word of God" (18:11). While the book of Acts clearly pictures the gospel spreading and churches being planted and multiplying, it also clearly emphasizes sound discipleship. In this vein we remember that the commission given to every believer is to *make disciples* of all the ethnicities. The church planters in Acts followed this part of the commission.

As happened in many cities mentioned in the book of Acts, Paul faced opposition from the Jews in Corinth, who brought him before the Roman authority. Gallio, however, would have nothing to do with the Jews' charges. Luke seems quite intentional in pointing out the numerous times when the government protected, or would not affirm accusations against, Paul and the new churches.

Overview of the Corinthian Church

Our study of the church plant in Corinth began when we noted the example that Aquila and Priscilla provided in Second Timothy 2:2: that of teaching "faithful men who [would] be able to teach others also." They provide another example as well: that of ordinary Christians starting churches where there are none. We learned that sent-out ones sometimes practice a trade (tentmaking) for economic reasons and sometimes to provide entrance to a place. In Corinth we found the direction of money flow remained consistent with that of other new churches in the New Testament: away from the new church. We also examined yet another example of the person-of-peace model being followed in the book of Acts. We took note that God can use people who are sometimes fearful. And we saw that Paul taught the Word of God in Corinth for eighteen months.

Paul departed from Corinth with Aquila and Priscilla, leaving them in Ephesus as he continued on to Jerusalem and Antioch. Thus Paul completed his second missionary journey, having left churches in Philippi, Thessalonica and Corinth.

10

THE CHURCH IN EPHESUS

Acts 18:23–20:38

Ephesus had been on Paul's mind for some time. At the beginning of Paul's second missionary journey, he had tried to go to Asia, where Ephesus was, but he had been forbidden by the Holy Spirit to evangelize the area at that time (see Acts 16:6). Then at the end of his second missionary journey, on his way to Jerusalem, Paul stopped by Ephesus and left Priscilla and Aquila there. He "entered the synagogue and reasoned with the Jews" (18:19), who asked him to stay for a longer time. He declined at that time but told them that he would return if God willed.

Finally, Paul was led by the Lord to minister in Ephesus. In this chapter we are going to look at the church he planted there—the ninth church in our study of the book of Acts—but first we will take a look at what finally led to Paul's arrival in this city.

Mentoring a New Worker

> And having spent some time [in Antioch], he left and passed successively through the Galatian region and Phrygia, strengthening all the disciples.
>
> Now a Jew named Apollos, an Alexandrian by birth, an eloquent man, came to Ephesus; and he was mighty in the

143

Scriptures. This man had been instructed in the way of the Lord; and being fervent in spirit, he was speaking and teaching accurately the things concerning Jesus, being acquainted only with the baptism of John; and he began to speak out boldly in the synagogue. But when Priscilla and Aquila heard him, they took him aside and explained to him the way of God more accurately. And when he wanted to go across to Achaia, the brethren encouraged him and wrote to the disciples to welcome him; and when he had arrived, he greatly helped those who had believed through grace, for he powerfully refuted the Jews in public, demonstrating by the Scriptures that Jesus was the Christ. (Acts 18:23–28)

A brother named Apollos came to Ephesus, where Priscilla and Aquila were now living. He was "mighty in the Scriptures," having been "instructed in the way of the Lord," and he was "fervent in spirit," or the Spirit. When he began speaking out boldly in the synagogue in Ephesus, Priscilla and Aquila "took him aside and explained to him the way of God more accurately."

Paul had earlier invested in the lives of Aquila and Priscilla, staying with them in Corinth several years before this time. These two now poured into Apollos here in Ephesus. Apollos wanted to go to Achaia (Corinth), and "the brethren encouraged him and wrote to the disciples to welcome him."

Just as Barnabas had opened doors for Saul of Tarsus, so now the brethren facilitated ministry opportunities for Apollos. Paul had discipled Aquila and Priscilla in one-on-two mentoring, and Aquila and Priscilla mentored Apollos, apparently in two-on-one mentoring similar to that which Paul had used with them. Apollos now went on to disciple believers in Corinth (see 1 Cor. 1:12; 3:6). From Paul to Aquila and Priscilla, to Apollos, to the disciples in Corinth—this made four generations of disciples.[1]

Did You Receive the Spirit?

> It happened that while Apollos was at Corinth, Paul passed through the upper country and came to Ephesus, and found some disciples. He said to them, "Did you receive the Holy Spirit when you believed?" And they said to him, "No, we have not even heard whether there is a Holy Spirit." And he said, "Into what then were you baptized?" And they said, "Into John's baptism." Paul said, "John baptized with the baptism of repentance, telling the people to believe in Him who was coming after him, that is, in Jesus." When they heard this, they were baptized in the name of the Lord Jesus. And when Paul had laid his hands upon them, the Holy Spirit came on them, and they began speaking with tongues and prophesying. There were in all about twelve men. (Acts 19:1–7)

Reception of the Holy Spirit characterizes those who have truly believed.

Paul began his third missionary journey as he had the second: by returning to the churches in Galatia and "strengthening all the disciples" (18:23).[2] Upon leaving Galatia he arrived in Ephesus, where he found a group of about twelve men. We are not told what led Paul to question these men, but he began by asking them, "Did you receive the Holy Spirit when you believed?" They responded in the negative, and Paul asked, "Into what then were you baptized?" Upon learning that they had been baptized into John's baptism, Paul began with John's baptism and from there led them to faith in Jesus.

Several insights can be gained by reflecting on Paul's questions to these men. First, reception of the Holy Spirit characterizes those who have truly believed. In Acts 1 we read that the apostles were promised the baptism of the Holy Spirit, resulting in power to be witnesses (see 1:5, 8). At the moment of salvation, all believers are placed in the body of Christ, and all receive the Holy Spirit, according to First Corinthians 12:13. This emphasizes a regenerate church membership. If church planters are not careful about people's salvation, they may find themselves trying to start churches with members who have made some lesser commitment, but who do not have the Holy Spirit.

The Holy Spirit produces the fruit of the Spirit in believers' lives (see Gal. 5:22–23), which makes the Christian life contagious. The surrounding community can see the transformation of the new believer and will know by his or her example that God is able to change lives. Jesus described the Holy Spirit's presence in a believer as "rivers of living water" (John 7:38). Paul's example here is extremely important for the church planter today: sent-out ones must make sure that new people are genuinely saved and have experienced the transformation that comes by the Spirit.[3] If people do not have the Spirit, they do not belong to Christ and are still in their sin (see Rom. 8:9).

Paul's questions to these men also highlight the wisdom of beginning a work by asking people questions. In the book of Acts, those sharing the good news often listen to people before speaking. In Acts 2 Peter listens: he hears that he and the other disciples are being accused of drunkenness and so begins talking to the people about not being drunk. In Acts 3 Peter listens: he hears that people are amazed, so he begins his work among them by asking, "Why are you amazed?" (3:12). Listening preceded sharing. Here in Ephesus Paul took the time to ask questions and to determine where his listeners were spiritually, and then he began presenting the gospel right where they were.

Finally, in Paul's response to these disciples of John the Baptist, notice that baptism was to follow faith in Jesus. This had been the norm since Acts 2. However, here in Acts 19 we encounter people for the first time who had been baptized before they genuinely were converted. These people, after hearing Paul's questions and truly believing in Jesus, were then baptized into the name of Jesus. This could be seen as rebaptism, but their first baptism was not an example of believer's baptism, which follows repentance and faith in Jesus Christ.

For those who were baptized as infants or in some other way baptized before conversion, this passage suggests that such baptisms do not take the place of a baptism that follows trusting Jesus for salvation. The baptisms of these men in Acts 19 and the gifts that follow speak to the unity of the body of Christ.[4]

Dialogue and Persuasion

> And [Paul] entered the synagogue and continued speaking out boldly for three months, reasoning and persuading them about the kingdom of God. (19:8)

The gifts and personality of a gospel presenter may affect how the gospel is shared.

After speaking to these men, Paul entered the synagogue and spoke out boldly about the kingdom of God. The verbs used here to describe Paul's sharing are insightful. The word *reasoning,* used in Acts 19:8, is the source of the English word *dialogue.*[5] This word is also used to describe Paul's evangelism in the synagogues in Thessalonica, Athens and Corinth, and it will be used to describe Paul's sharing later on in Ephesus in the school of Tyrannus. It pictures a back-and-forth conversation more than a one-sided lecture.

Paul was also "persuading," which included a desire to have his listeners respond positively to the message he proclaimed. The book of Acts uses other verbs to describe sharing the good news: *testified* (2:40), *preach* (10:42), *preaching the good news* (8:12), *witness* (see 1:8; 2:32), *proclaim* (9:20), *speaking* (11:19) and *talking and arguing* (9:29). The gifts and personality of the presenter may affect how he or she shares the gospel. The attitude and situation of the hearer may influence the worker's preferred way to share. There is more than one way to share the good news.

Meeting in a School

> When some were becoming hardened and disobedient, speaking evil of the Way before the people, [Paul] withdrew from [the synagogue] and took away the disciples, reasoning daily in the school of Tyrannus. This took place for two years, so that all who lived in Asia heard the word of the Lord, both Jews and Greeks. (19:9–10)

The response in the synagogue in Ephesus was similar to that in other places: some were disobedient and began to speak against the Way. So Paul left the synagogue and went to a school, where he engaged people in dialogue and taught daily for two years.

This location for ministry is noteworthy. In Jerusalem the church had been started in the temple. The kinds of places most often mentioned as meeting places for churches are homes.[6] In Philippi the believers met by the riverside (see Acts 16:13) and in Athens in the marketplace (see 17:17). Now here in Ephesus they meet in a school.

The length of time that they met is also noteworthy. Two years are mentioned here, while later Paul describes his total time in Ephesus as "a period of three years" (20:31). The gospel spread throughout this region in only three years. This is the longest period that Paul stays anywhere in the book of Acts, but it is very short when compared to other church-planting work throughout church history.

The Gospel Spreading

> This took place for two years, so that all who lived in Asia heard the word of the Lord, both Jews and Greeks. (19:10)

During Paul's three-year period in Ephesus, "all who lived in Asia heard the word of the Lord." As we saw in chapter 4 of this book regarding Pisidian Antioch and in chapter 8 regarding Thessalonica, the book of Acts tells us that the gospel often spread throughout regions.

Paul's letter to the church in Colossae, another city in Asia, may provide insight into how the gospel spread through the province of Asia. Paul had never met the Colossians (see Col. 2:1), but Epaphras, a native of Colossae (see 4:12), had taken the gospel to them (see 1:7) and probably also to Laodicea and Hierapolis (see 4:12–13), which were close by. Epaphras is closely tied to Paul (see 1:7; Philem. 1:23), suggesting that Paul may have led him to faith in Christ during these years in

Ephesus. After coming to faith, Epaphras went home to Colossae and planted the church there and then planted churches in the nearby cities of Laodicea and Hierapolis.

Another example from these three years illustrates how the gospel spread. Paul mentions in First Corinthians 16:8 that he would "remain in Ephesus until Pentecost," connecting his writing of First Corinthians with his time in Ephesus (see Acts 19:10). Later, in First Corinthians 16, Paul writes, "The churches of Asia greet you" (16:19). Multiple churches existed in Asia by this time, and besides Ephesus, Paul is perhaps referring to Colossae and Laodicea.

Paul also sent greetings to the Corinthians from Aquila and Priscilla "with the church that is in their house" (16:19). The couple that Paul spent time with in Corinth now lived in Ephesus, and a church was meeting in their home there. They sent greetings from this church back to the Corinthians. Later Aquila and Priscilla returned to Italy, and when Paul wrote the church in Rome, he sent the couple a greeting and added, "Also greet the church that is in their house" (Rom. 16:5). After being mentored by Paul, wherever this couple moved, they started a church or had one meeting in their home. This is what we saw regarding the church in Antioch: whenever ordinary Christians went to a place that had no church, they started a new one.

We might wish for more details, but the text is clear: the gospel spread through the entire region of Asia during Paul's time in Ephesus.

Positives and Negatives

God was performing extraordinary miracles by the hands of Paul, so that handkerchiefs or aprons were even carried from his body to the sick, and the diseases left them and the evil spirits went out. But also some of the Jewish exorcists, who went from place to place, attempted to name over those who had the evil spirits the name of the Lord Jesus, saying, "I adjure you by Jesus whom Paul preaches." Seven sons of one Sceva, a Jewish chief priest, were doing this. And the evil spirit answered and said to them, "I recognize Jesus, and I know about Paul, but who are you?" And the man, in whom was the evil spirit, leaped on them and subdued all of them and overpowered them, so that they fled out of that house naked and wounded. This became known to all, both Jews and Greeks, who lived in Ephesus; and fear fell upon them all and the name of the Lord Jesus was being magnified. Many also of those who had believed kept coming, confessing and disclosing their practices. And many of those who practiced magic brought their books together and began burning them in the sight of everyone; and they counted up the price of them and found it fifty thousand pieces of silver. So the word of the Lord was growing mightily and prevailing. (Acts 19:11–20)

The powerful work in Ephesus was accompanied by very positive and very negative details. "God was performing extraordinary miracles by the hands of Paul," specifically causing diseases as well as evil spirits to leave people. From the beginning of Acts, healing and miracles are referred to by the word *signs* (see 2:22, 43; 4:30; 5:12; 6:8; 8:6; 14:3; 15:12), as they are in John's Gospel, where Christ's miracles are called signs because they point to His identity as God the Son.

In Romans Paul writes that these signs are an indication that his work has been of Christ (see 15:19). In Second Corinthians, written shortly after he left Ephesus, Paul refers to signs as that which authenticate his role as an apostle (see 12:12). So in a positive way, God established the work with signs.[7]

Another positive detail is that the new believers were burning their magic books at a cost of fifty thousand days' wages (see Acts 19:19)! They were willing to pay a price to follow Jesus and were taking their personal holiness seriously. Here is a beautiful picture of sound contextualization: as these new believers came to Christ, they rejected those things from their past and from their tradition that were inconsistent with the Word of God.[8]

Nothing in Acts suggests that Spirit-led ministers need be fearful of spirits, but dealing with evil spirits should not be something that one looks for or plays with.

The negative detail was related to one of the positives—the evil spirits going out of some. On a certain occasion Paul had commanded an evil spirit, in Jesus' name, to come out of a slave girl in Philippi (see 16:18).[9] This kind of endeavor was not stressed as a major part of Paul's ministry, but when faced with an evil spirit, Paul dealt with the situation in Jesus' name. Some, however, attempted to delve into an exorcism ministry based on Paul's authority, and it did not turn out so well. "The man, in whom was the evil spirit, leaped on them and subdued all of them and overpowered them, so that they fled out of that house naked and wounded" (19:16). Nothing in Acts suggests that Spirit-led ministers need be fearful of spirits, but this kind of ministry should not be something that one looks for or plays with.

Strengthening the Churches

After these things were finished, Paul purposed in the Spirit to go to Jerusalem after he had passed through Macedonia and Achaia, saying, "After I have been there, I must also see Rome." (Acts 19:21)

Shortly before leaving Ephesus Paul "purposed in the Spirit" to return to Macedonia and Achaia, strengthening the churches from his second missionary journey, and then to go to Jerusalem and afterward to Rome.

The details of his trip may not have come about as he expected, but Paul did do each of these things, suggesting that the Spirit had indeed guided his plans.[10] The major unexpected aspect of Paul's travels was his arriving in Rome as a prisoner, but unexpected happenings began with his leaving Ephesus following a riot. Leaving a city amidst opposition was normal for Paul, but what was unusual in Ephesus was that he had ministered three years prior to this opposition, which then forced his departure, and his departure came *after* he had planned the cities he would go to next.

When a church planter takes key individuals with him or her, it maximizes the benefit of a trip.

As his third missionary journey came to a close, Paul strengthened the earlier church plants. He began this third journey returning to and strengthening the churches from his first missionary journey (see 18:23); then after three years of ministry at Ephesus, where he planted the new church of this third journey, Paul returned to Macedonia (Philippi and Thessalonica) and Greece (Corinth), where churches had been planted on the second journey, as he had purposed in the Spirit (see 20:1–3).

During these travels "he was accompanied by Sopater of Berea, the son of Pyrrhus, and by Aristarchus and Secundus of the Thessalonians, and Gaius of Derbe, and Timothy, and Tychicus and Trophimus of Asia" (Acts 20:4). As he finished his third missionary journey, Paul was still mentoring leaders from the first journey (Derbe), the second journey (Berea and Thessalonica) and the third journey (Asia). What an excellent example for church planters today: taking key individuals with us as we travel maximizes the benefit of a trip.

Elders/Overseers/Pastors

> Paul had decided to sail past Ephesus so that he would not have to spend time in Asia; for he was hurrying to be in Jerusalem, if possible, on the day of Pentecost.
>
> From Miletus he sent to Ephesus and called to him the elders of the church. And when they had come to him, he said to them,
>
> "You yourselves know, from the first day that I set foot in Asia, how I was with you the whole time, serving the Lord with all humility and with tears and with trials which came upon me through the plots of the Jews; how I did not shrink from declaring to you anything that was profitable, and teaching you publicly and from house to house, solemnly testifying to both Jews and Greeks of repentance toward God and faith in our Lord Jesus Christ. "And now, behold, bound by the Spirit, I am on my way to Jerusalem, not knowing what will happen to me there, except that the Holy Spirit solemnly testifies to me in every city, saying that bonds and afflictions await me. But I do not consider my life of any account as dear to myself, so that I may finish my course and the ministry which I received from the Lord Jesus, to testify solemnly of the gospel of the grace of God.

"And now, behold, I know that all of you, among whom I went about preaching the kingdom, will no longer see my face. Therefore, I testify to you this day that I am innocent of the blood of all men. For I did not shrink from declaring to you the whole purpose of God. Be on guard for yourselves and for all the flock, among which the Holy Spirit has made you overseers, to shepherd the church of God which He purchased with His own blood. I know that after my departure savage wolves will come in among you, not sparing the flock; and from among your own selves men will arise, speaking perverse things, to draw away the disciples after them. Therefore be on the alert, remembering that night and day for a period of three years I did not cease to admonish each one with tears." (Acts 20:16–31)

Time was becoming short, because Paul wanted to be in Jerusalem on the day of Pentecost. For that reason he did not go into the city of Ephesus as he passed by it but rather called for the church elders to meet him at Miletus.

Several important insights come from his words with the elders. First, note that Paul called the elders *overseers*, or *bishops*, and instructed them to shepherd, or pastor,[11] the church. As we've seen with a number of the new churches, in the New Testament the titles *elder*, *overseer* and *shepherd* are repeatedly attributed to the same group of people.[12] The plural form of the word *elders* is typically used in the New Testament, reminding us that it is wise to have a plurality of leaders both for the health of a new church and to prepare new churches to multiply.

Paul called for a response of repentance and faith from these leaders (see 20:21). He determined before them to finish his course (see 20:24), which is one reason he was able to do just that many years later (see 2 Tim. 4:8). Paul desired to finish the ministry that he had received from the Lord Jesus (see

Acts 20:24), and this goal is worthy for every church planter today (see Col. 4:17). Paul wanted to be innocent of the blood of all men (see Acts 20:26), calling to mind the powerful challenge of Ezekiel 33:8: if a leader does not warn the wicked, that leader will be responsible for the wicked man's blood. Paul told the elders that he had declared to the churches "the whole purpose of God" (Acts 20:27). He told them that pastors and elders were necessary in the church because savage wolves would arise from among the churches and draw people away from the faith (see 20:29–30). This reminds us that church planters must never be naïve, because Scripture has warned us about this (see 2 Pet. 2:1). Paul finished his words to the elders of Ephesus by telling them that he was confident that he had worked hard, night and day (see Acts 20:31).[13]

Commended to God and His Word

> "And now I commend you to God and to the word of His grace, which is able to build you up and to give you the inheritance among all those who are sanctified. I have coveted no one's silver or gold or clothes. You yourselves know that these hands ministered to my own needs and to the men who were with me. In everything I showed you that by working hard in this manner you must help the weak and remember the words of the Lord Jesus, that He Himself said, 'It is more blessed to give than to receive.'"
>
> When [Paul] had said these things, he knelt down and prayed with them all. And they began to weep aloud and embraced Paul, and repeatedly kissed him, grieving especially over the word which he had spoken, that they would not see his face again. And they were accompanying him to the ship. (20:32–38)

Paul commended the church to two things: "to God and to the word of His grace," which was able to build them up and give them the inheritance among all those who are sanctified. This calls to mind how Paul had commended the churches from his first missionary journey "to the Lord in whom they had believed" (Acts 14:23). Paul similarly closes the book of Romans by referring to "Him who is able to establish [the believers] . . . by the Scriptures" (16:25–26).

The church planter must be careful that new believers are genuinely converted—that they have God. He must also be careful that the believers have God's Word and know how to live by it. When these two standards are in place, the church planter can leave a new congregation and be assured of their growth. In the book of Acts, the work was not built on the church planter but on God and His Word.

In the New Testament, leaving does not mean deserting. Paul later wrote to the Ephesian church (see Eph. 1:1) and continued to visit the believers or send others to them (see 1 Tim. 1:3).

Overview of the Ephesian Church

We began our examination of the church plant in Ephesus noting how Aquila and Priscilla mentored, or discipled, Apollos just as Paul had mentored or discipled them. Another unique insight we gained from this church plant is that church members must be truly regenerate and genuinely have the Spirit's power in their lives. We saw that there is more than one way to share the good news. We also saw that Paul met in a school for two years.

We noted once again the common threads: The gospel spread through the entire region of Asia, perhaps when

Epaphras and others like him were converted under Paul's ministry in Ephesus and then took the gospel home and began churches in the towns and cities of the region. Paul completed his third missionary journey by strengthening the churches that had been planted during his second journey and discipling leaders whom he had found along the way in all three journeys. Paul challenged the elders who had been established in the Ephesian church, and he commended the church to God and to His Word.

Paul left the elders in Ephesus and returned to the church at Antioch, from where he traveled on to Jerusalem. The third missionary journey of the book of Acts was complete, and the ninth church plant was left in Ephesus.

EPILOGUE

Nine descriptions of church plants. Common threads woven through each story. Unique insights found along the way. The Holy Spirit waits to use these stories to guide church planters today.

The lack of clear commands regarding church planting is obvious: not once was a command given that this or that model was to be the only normative way to plant churches. But the New Testament does describe *church planting where the gospel is not* as a primary task of sent-out ones.

If one feels led to church planting, surely he will want to carefully consider the book of the New Testament that deals with that specific topic nine times. The New Testament, in the book of Acts, clearly describes nine church plants. Since the Scriptures are our norm for faith *and practice*, and since no other writing is God-breathed as is the Word of God, we must put the Scripture's descriptions of church planting on a higher level of authority than those of any other source on the topic.

We saw the common threads in several of the church plants: *Prayer,* on the part of both the church-planting team and the church that was planted, was a major emphasis in the church at Jerusalem, and it was mentioned in Antioch, Pisidian Antioch, Lystra, Iconium, Philippi and Ephesus. In Jerusalem *evangelism began with those who had already been exposed to God's Word.* The same was noted in Pisidian Antioch, Iconium, Thessalonica, Corinth and Ephesus. *The gospel was presented on the authority of Scripture* in Jerusalem, Pisidian Antioch, Lystra and Thessalonica. The gospel consists of the good news of the death of Jesus for our sins and of His burial and resurrection according to the Scriptures, calling for a response of faith and repentance. Those who repented and believed were baptized.

The role of the Holy Spirit to convict and save was woven into the accounts in Jerusalem, Antioch and Thessalonica. The emphasis on discipleship was noted in Jerusalem, Antioch, Pisidian Antioch, Iconium, Lystra, Philippi, Thessalonica, Corinth and Ephesus: in each of the nine church plants in Acts! *Opposition* was noted in Jerusalem, Pisidian Antioch, Iconium, Lystra, Philippi, Thessalonica, Corinth and Ephesus. *Departing and then returning to strengthen the church* and/or leaders was noted in Pisidian Antioch, Iconium, Lystra, Philippi, Thessalonica, Corinth and Ephesus.

Equipping leaders for and from the new congregations was another common thread found in each of the nine church plants in Acts. A *plan, or custom*, was noted in Pisidian Antioch, Iconium, Thessalonica, Corinth and Ephesus, while departure from the plan at times was obvious: a plan can be good, but God is our guide. We saw the *multiplication of churches* in Jerusalem, Antioch, Thessalonica and Ephesus. The characteristics of a *healthy church* were specifically noted in Jerusalem, Antioch, Philippi and Thessalonica. These common threads were woven repeatedly through the book of Acts.

While not mentioned in all the church plants in Acts, unique insights were woven into some of the narratives and are significant for the consideration of church planters today: The Holy Spirit's guidance was common, although He guided in unique ways. We saw the Holy Spirit's filling for every believer in Jerusalem and Pisidian Antioch and noted it as normative in the rest of the New Testament. The issue of heart language was noted in Jerusalem and in Lystra. In Jerusalem speaking in the people's heart language created a positive bridge, and in Lystra the disciples found not knowing the heart language to be a surmountable challenge that they overcame.

Contextualization was defined as standing against unscriptural practices as well as the positive incorporation of appropriate words and actions from culture into church planting. The places where churches met were distinct in each city. We saw the person-of-peace model used in Pisidian Antioch, Philippi and Corinth, demonstrating that the model commanded by Jesus for the Twelve and the seventy did not stop with the Gospels.

A creation-to-Christ story, providing an overview story of the Old Testament to give context for a gospel presentation, was used in Jerusalem and Pisidian Antioch. Paul worked as a tentmaker when circumstances required. The direction of the money flow was noted in Antioch and Philippi. While this topic is not mentioned in every church in Acts, the direction of funds was noted as consistent throughout the New Testament.

These unique insights are not found in every church plant in the book of Acts, but the Spirit chose to include them in Scripture for our normative practice. The church planter today should prayerfully consider each of them as he makes plans and evaluates practices.

As church planters today, we must prayerfully seek the Lord's guidance through the Spirit and the Word in our church-planting work. Our study in this book is just the water to prime the pump. May the Spirit provide a stream of guidance from His Word as we, in our day, continue church planting by the Book.

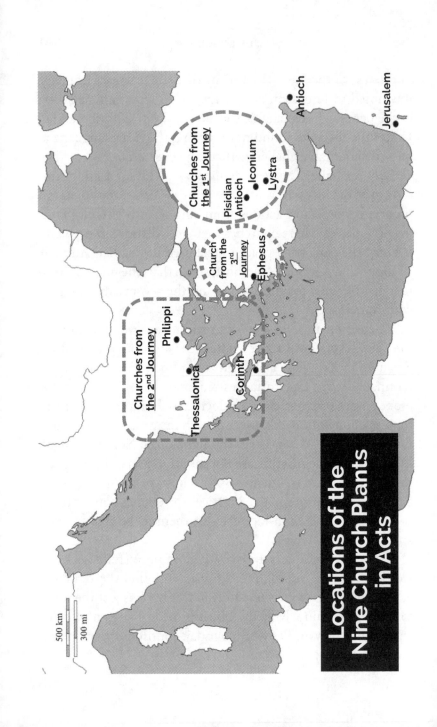

Locations of the Nine Church Plants in Acts

Antioch

Jerusalem

Churches from the 1st Journey

Pisidian Antioch

Iconium

Lystra

Church from the 3rd Journey

Ephesus

Churches from the 2nd Journey

Philippi

Thessalonica

Corinth

500 km

300 mi

NOTES

Introduction

1. Scripture begins calling our attention to distinct people groups at the beginning of the Bible in Genesis 10:5: "The nations were separated into their lands, every one according to his language, according to their families, into their nations." This theme is found at the other end of Scripture with the vision of "a great multitude which no one could count, from every nation and all tribes and peoples and tongues, standing before the throne" (Rev. 7:9). Attention to people groups is paramount for all followers of Jesus, because our marching orders are to make disciples of all ethnicities (see Matt. 28:18–20; in 28:19 "all the nations" is a translation of *panta ta ethne* [πάντα τὰ ἔθνη], from which we get our word *ethnicity*).

2. This passion of God for "all the families of the earth" (Gen. 12:3) is clearly seen in Abraham's call and continues through both the Old and New Testaments (see Exod. 7:5; 1 Kings 8:60; Ps. 67:1–7; Isa. 49:6; John 3:16; Rom. 10:13–15; Rev. 7:9).

3. The English word *missionary* comes from a Latin root meaning "sent out." Since the word *missionary* can have negative connotations in some parts of the world, I prefer to use its core meaning: "sent-out ones." Sent-out ones,

in my understanding, are those in the body of Christ who have been gifted and called by the Holy Spirit (see 1 Cor. 12:27–28; Eph. 4:11) to go where the gospel is not (see Rom. 15:20–21), to herald the gospel (see Mark 1:14; 3:14; 13:10), to make disciples (see Matt. 28:19), and to establish New Testament churches before moving to the next place (see Acts 13–20). For a more thorough discussion that also describes the relationship of the term *missionary*, or "sent-out one," to the word *apostle*, see chapter 6, where we come to it more naturally as we work our way through the narrative flow of Acts.

4.   Immediately after the description of Paul's first visit to Jerusalem in Acts 9:26–30 comes Acts 9:31, which mentions "the church throughout all Judea and Galilee and Samaria." This visit is the time referred to in the introduction as perhaps little more than four to five years after the ascension. (This timing can be concluded from several New Testament passages: The letter to the Galatians appears to have been written to the churches of Paul's first journey and seems to precede the Jerusalem council, which took place in AD 48 or 49. According to Galatians 2:1, Paul was converted fourteen years before his visit to Jerusalem, around AD 34 to 36. His visit to Jerusalem happened three years after his conversion [see 1:18], which would put the visit around AD 36 to 39— approximately four to five years after the ascension.)

5.   On his journey to Jerusalem after his third missionary journey, Paul stayed in Caesarea with Philip the evangelist, and the description of his time there seems to indicate a church (see Acts 21:8–14). We are not, however, told specifically about a church in Caesarea.

Chapter 1

1. The Greek word translated "serve" is the verb form of the noun translated as "deacon."

2. Luke 22 begins with the clarification that the Feast of Unleavened Bread was called the Passover. In 22:15–16, Jesus speaks of the Passover being fulfilled, which His suffering on the cross accomplishes. Just as the original Passover lamb spared a home a visit by the death angel (see Exod. 12), so Jesus' death as the Lamb of God provides life for all who believe.

3. Leviticus 23:16 says, "You shall count fifty days" after the Feast of Unleavened Bread. The word *Pentecost* means "fiftieth."

4. As mentioned in the introduction, narrative passages such as this one in Acts 2 (which highlights Israel's historical narrative as well) provide principles and insights that the Holy Spirit may apply to church-planting teams today, as distinguished from prescriptive commands for all situations.

5. The Greek word *chronos* (χρόνος) refers primarily to chronological time. The word for "time" in Ephesians 5:15–16 is *kairos* (καιρός), which can refer to "strategic opportunities."

6. There is another reference in Second Corinthians 3:7 to *glory*, speaking of the glory of Moses' face, but this refers specifically to Exodus 33:9 and 34:34–35, which refer to the pillar of cloud and to Moses' face shining because of God's presence.

7. In Acts 1:4–5 Jesus describes the promise of the Father
    as the believers being "baptized with the Holy Spirit,"
    which would happen not many days after Jesus left for
    heaven. First Corinthians 12:13 provides the clearest
    New Testament explanation of being baptized by the
    Spirit: at the moment of our salvation, the Holy Spirit
    puts the believer into the body of Christ, and the Spirit
    comes to live inside the person so that his or her "body is
    a temple of the Holy Spirit who is in" us (6:19).

8. Acts 11:17 clearly states that the members of Cornelius'
    household believed first before they were filled with the
    Holy Spirit.

9. The Greek word translated "language" in Acts 2:6 and 8
    is *dialektos* (διάλεκτος), from which we get our English
    word *dialect*.

10. One can see the emphasis throughout the book of Acts
    on the cross and the resurrection in Acts 3:15, 26; 4:10;
    5:30; 10:40; 13:30, 33–34 and 17:31.

11. The Greek word translated "gospel" (*euangelion*,
    εὐαγγέλιον) literally means "good news."

12. In Acts 14:4 and 14 Paul and Barnabas are called "apos-
    tles," which is the noun form of the verb translated "to
    send" or "to send out." Apostles are "ones sent out." We
    will discuss the term "sent-out ones" in more detail in
    chapter 6 of this book.

13. Greek manuscripts from the sixth century begin to add
    the word *church* to Acts 2:47. While the word is not in
    the oldest manuscripts, it seems to explain the mean-
    ing of the phrase "to their number." Those who believed

Peter's message of the gospel were added to the church by repentance, faith and baptism.

Chapter 2

1. The Greek word used in Acts 2:42 for "fellowship" is *koinōnia* (κοινωνία).

2. Acts 2:46 mentions the new believers "taking their meals together with gladness," which seems to picture fellowship, while this statement in 2:42, "the breaking of bread," seems to refer rather to the Lord's Supper.

3. Baptism is commanded in Matthew 28:19 and Acts 2:38 and the Lord's Supper in Luke 22:19 and First Corinthians 11:23–26.

4. The pattern of church growth in the book of Acts can be seen in 2:41, 4:4, 9:31, 12:24, 16:5, 19:20 and 21:20. If growth is not the experience of some church planters, however, they should be careful to keep Scripture as their norm and not assume that their experience takes priority over Scripture.

5. Aquila and Priscilla provide a wonderful example of the impact that those we invest in can have. Paul had stayed with them in Corinth (see Acts 18:2–3) and had so mentored them, or so invested in their lives, that after they moved to Ephesus (see 18:18–19), a church met in their home (see 1 Cor. 16:19). When they moved back to Rome (where they were originally from), a church met in their home again (see Rom. 16:5). See a fuller description of this in chapter 9 of this book.

6.   The verses in Acts that mention believers gathering in homes (see 2:46; 5:42; 10:22; 12:12; 16:32, 40; 18:7; 20:20) suggest that homes were not just places in which churches began but were normal ongoing meeting places for the churches.

7.   Signs are mentioned in the Jerusalem church as being done at the hands of the apostles (see Acts 2:43; 5:12) and through Stephen (see 6:8). In Samaria signs were performed by Philip (see 8:6–7). On his first missionary journey, Paul blinded Elymas the magician in Cyprus (see 13:8–11), signs and wonders were performed in Iconium (see 14:1–3), and Paul healed a lame man in Lystra (see 14:8–10). On his second journey Paul told a spirit to come out of a slave girl at Philippi (see 16:16–18), resulting in his arrest. On his third journey "God was performing extraordinary miracles by the hands of Paul" (19:11), with people being healed and evil spirits going out of them. On his journey to Jerusalem, Paul restored a young man who fell from a third-floor window and "was picked up dead" (20:9; see also 20:10). On his journey to Rome, Publius's father was healed, and others were cured (see 28:8–9). No mention is made of signs or healings in Pisidian Antioch, Derbe, Thessalonica, Berea, Athens, Macedonia, Greece or Caesarea. While the book of Acts makes no mention of signs taking place in Corinth, Paul later writes to the Corinthian church, "The signs of a true apostle were performed among you with all perseverance, by signs and wonders and miracles" (2 Cor. 12:12). Signs are mentioned several times in the book of Acts, but in many cities discussed in Acts they are not mentioned.

8. It should be noted that Jesus' description of the Good Samaritan lacks the miraculous element found in Jesus' healings and in the healings in Acts but rather indicates healing in this instance through physical care and medicine.

9. Believers are found in jail, prison or captivity in Acts 4, 5, 8, 12, 16, 21, 22, 23, 24, 25, 26 and 28.

10. At times in the book of Acts, believers flee in response to persecution (see 9:25, 30; 17:10, 14)—as Jesus had taught in Matthew 10:23—while at other times (see 4:29–31) they seem to be led to stay where they are. It seems that the Holy Spirit gives guidance in each situation. This topic is discussed more fully in chapter 5 of this book (see also mention of it in chapter 8).

11. The boldness of the new believers in Acts 4:29–31 in the face of persecution reminds us of the victory over Satan by believers described in Revelation 12:11: "And they overcame him because of the blood of the Lamb and because of the word of their testimony, and they did not love their life even when faced with death."

12. See more detailed discussion on the interchangeable use of the terms *overseer* (which can be translated "bishop"), *elder* and *shepherd* (which can be translated "pastor") in chapter 5 of this book.

13. The word *serve* in Acts 6:2 comes from the Greek verb *diakoneō* (διακονέω), from which our English word *deacon* comes.

14. Apollos was a leader at Corinth (see 1 Cor. 3:6) who was originally from Alexandria (see Acts 18:24, 27).

Chapter 3

1. This story in Acts 8 is an example of the negative side of
    contextualization. For an example of the positive side of
    contextualization, see the discussion of Acts 11:20 later
    in this chapter.

2. This method of the sent-out one seeking, or "filtering"
    for, the ones whom God has prepared to listen to the
    gospel is known by some as the person-of-peace model.
    It is based on Jesus' teaching in Matthew 10:5–14, Mark
    6:7–11, Luke 9:1–5 and Luke 10:1–11, in which the
    disciples are instructed to go out and preach the gospel,
    looking for a "man of peace" (Luke 10:6)—someone who
    is open to the gospel and in whose home they can stay.
    We will discuss the person-of-peace model in chapter 4
    of this book.

3. We saw this same kind of broad gospel sowing (whereby
    the people heard of the wonders of God before they ac-
    tually heard the gospel message) in the Jerusalem church.

4. How could Philip be an example to church members
    today of being involved in both planting a new church
    across town and in getting the gospel to unreached
    people groups around the world (see Acts 8:4, 26, 39–40;
    21:8)?

5. The word *encouragement,* used to describe Barnabas the
    encourager in Acts 4:36, comes from the same root as the
    Greek *paraklētos* (παράκλητος), which is used of the Holy
    Spirit in John 16.

6. We find the term *Jesus Christ* used by church planters
    speaking to the lost in Acts 2:38, 3:6, 4:10, 9:34 and

10:36. While the term *Lord Jesus* has been used six times up to this point in Acts (chapter 11), most uses of that name were among believers (possible exceptions would be in 4:33, where it says that the apostles were telling people about the resurrection of the "Lord Jesus," and perhaps in 9:17, when Ananias speaks to Saul after Saul's Damascus road experience and says that "the Lord Jesus" has sent him).

7. The term *Lord Jesus* is used in Acts 16:31 and 19:17. The term *Lord Jesus Christ* is used in 20:21 and 28:31.

8. We can see the emphasis on the work of the Holy Spirit throughout the book of Acts in Acts 1:5, 8; 2:4, 38; 4:8, 31; 5:32; 6:3, 10; 7:55; 8:29, 39; 9:17, 31; 10:19, 44, 45, 47; 11:24; 13:2, 4, 9, 52; 15:8; 16:6; 19:2, 6 and 20:28.

9. I see Romans 4:20–21 as one definition of faith: Abraham "did not waver in unbelief but grew strong in faith, giving glory to God, and being fully assured that what God had promised, He was able also to perform."

10. In Paul's letters to the churches, we see four major prayer requests that he makes of the believers. In Colossians 4:3–4 Paul asks the believers to pray (1) for an open door for the Word. He also asks them to pray (2) that the workers would make the message clear, and in Ephesians 6:19 he similarly asks that utterance be given in the opening of their mouths "to make known with boldness the mystery of the gospel." In Second Thessalonians 3:1–2 Paul asks the church to pray (3) "that the word of the Lord will spread rapidly" and (4) that the workers would be rescued from evil men. These four prayers have

been used throughout church history and can be used by sent-out ones today.

11. Paul and Barnabas spent a year with "the church," which here in Acts 11:26 is speaking of the church in Antioch. We noted in the introduction of this book that we are dealing specifically with those congregations that are expressly called churches in the New Testament.

12. In Acts 11:24, which refers to "considerable numbers" being saved, and Acts 11:26, which refers to "considerable numbers" being discipled, Luke uses different forms of the same two words, *ochlos ikanos* (ὄχλος ἱκανὸς).

13. Both Acts 11:26, in which the apostles "taught" the new believers, and Matthew 28:20, in which Jesus commands His followers to be "teaching" people to obey Him, use the word *didaskō* (διδασκω). Acts 11:26 uses an aorist active infinitive for this word, while Matthew 28:20 uses a present active participle.

14. The word *Christian* is used twice in Acts (see 11:26; 26:28), and both times it is used by others to refer to believers. The Greek word is used only three times in the New Testament: in the two places in Acts mentioned above and in First Peter 4:16. The passage in Peter is the only time we see in Scripture a Christian calling himself by that name. While *Christian* is a wonderful term to describe followers of Jesus, we should be quick to notice that it is used only three times in the New Testament.

15. *Disciples* is a common term used to describe believers in the book of Acts (see 6:1, 2, 7; 9:1, 10, 19, 26, 36, 38; 11:26, 29; 13:52; 14:20, 21, 22, 28; 15:10; 16:1; 18:23, 27; 19:9, 30; 20:1, 30; 21:4, 16).

16. *Believer* is used several times in Acts but more often by Paul in his epistles (see Acts 5:14; 10:45; 16:1; 2 Cor. 6:15; Gal. 3:9; 1 Thess. 1:7; 2:10; 1 Tim. 4:10; 5:16; 6:2).

17. Believers *brothers* or *brethren* is used to describe fellow believers in Acts 1:15, 16; 6:3; 9:17, 30; 10:23; 11:1, 12, 29; 12:17; 14:2; 15:1, 3, 7, 13, 22, 23, 32, 33, 36, 40; 16:2, 40; 17:6, 10, 14; 18:18, 27; 21:7, 17, 20; 22:13 and 28:14, 15. The term is also used in other places by Jews to describe fellow Jews.

18. See further description of the direction of the new churches' money flow in chapters 7 and 9 of this book.

19. One can cross reference the term *prophets and teachers* in Acts 13:1 with Ephesians 4:11 where, after apostles (sent-out ones) and prophets, pastor-teachers are listed, along with evangelists. Each of these is given to the church "for the equipping of the saints for the work of service, to the building up of the body of Christ" (4:12). Prophets and teachers are also found in First Corinthians 12:28–29.

20. The Holy Spirit had called Barnabas and Saul to the work of advancing the gospel (see Acts 13:2), and they were sent out by Him (see 13:4). The church "released" (*apoluō*, ἀπολύω) them—freed them, or let them go.

21. The conclusion that Paul, in his statement regarding "the churches of Judea" (Gal. 1:22), is referring to the period in which the Jerusalem church was multiplying into nearby regions assumes that Galatians 2:1–10 (Paul's trip to Jerusalem to tell the leaders of his preaching to the Gentiles) refers to Acts 11 (Peter's trip to Jerusalem to

report to the council of leaders regarding his ministry to Cornelius). We have already noted that Acts 9:31 mentions "the church throughout all Judea and Galilee and Samaria." The church universal was in all these areas but likely was made up of many local churches, not just the local church in Jerusalem.

22. We will discuss the concept of church growth in greater detail in chapter 7 of this book, where we will see additional new churches in Antioch and the surrounding area.

23. Although only three of the five characteristics of a healthy church (discipleship, ministry, and evangelism and missions) are seen obviously in the Antioch church, we assume that worship and fellowship, the other two characteristics, were present also, even though they are not described as clearly in Acts 11 as in other places in Acts.

Chapter 4

1. We see in Acts 13:4–12 that the first stop on Paul and Barnabas' missionary journey was the island of Cyprus. The text does not tell us whether or not a church was planted there. Barnabas would later return to Cyprus.

2. Acts 4:36 tells us that Barnabas was "a Levite of Cyprian birth." Could the fact that Barnabas and Paul went first to Cyprus on their missionary journey reflect a "go home and tell" mindset on the part of Barnabas (see Luke 8:39)? There is tremendous potential in every believer accepting responsibility for taking the gospel to his or her family, people group and hometown.

3. In Acts 11:30, 12:25, 13:2 and 13:7, Barnabas is named before Paul. Beginning in 13:13 Paul is listed first, which becomes the normal pattern for the remainder of Acts.

4. See the discussion on Acts 2 in chapter 1 of this book regarding broad seed sowing—preparing people for the gospel before they hear it preached.

5. Each of the references listed here as mentioning Jesus and Paul proclaiming the gospel (see Matt. 4:23; 9:35; 24:14; Mark 1:14; Gal. 2:2; 1 Thess. 2:9) uses the verb *kērussō* (κηρύσσω), which means "to announce like a herald," and the noun *euangelion* (εὐαγγέλιον), the word translated "gospel." For other passages that highlight Paul being sent to preach the gospel, consider Acts 16:10; Acts 20:24; Romans 15:16, 19; First Corinthians 1:17 and First Timothy 1:11.

6. The following New Testament passages show that the Servant mentioned several times by the prophet Isaiah is Jesus: Matthew 12:17–21, Romans 15:12 (referencing Isa. 42:1–9), John 8:12 (referencing Isa. 49:1–6), Matthew 26:67, Mark 15:19 (referencing Isa. 50:4–11), Matthew 8:17 and First Peter 2:24 (referencing Isa. 52:13–53:12).

7. The verb *ektinassō* (ἐκτινάσσω), "to shake off," is found in the New Testament four times (see Matt. 10:14; Mark 6:11; Acts 13:51; 18:6), each of which seems to deal with the person-of-peace model.

8. John clarified what Jesus meant by "rivers of living water" in John 7:38: "This He spoke of the Spirit, whom those who believed in Him were to receive" (7:39). This made it clear that the Spirit was for all who believed in Jesus.

Chapter 5

1. The Greek word for "a multitude" or "a great number" is *plēthos* (πλῆθος).

2. The Greek word for "many" or "large" is *polus* (πολύς).

3. See the discussion on signs and wonders in chapter 2 of this book.

4. In the passages that tell of the three church plants of Paul's second missionary journey (Philippi, Thessalonica and Corinth), the word for "miracle" or "sign" or "wonder" is not used, but supernatural occurrences did take place. Paul cast a spirit out of a slave girl (see Acts 16:18), and God sent an earthquake to release Paul and Silas from jail (see 16:25–26).

5. When Jesus sent out the Twelve, they were to "proclaim the kingdom of God and to perform healing" (Luke 9:2). If the example of Jesus in the Gospels and of those in Acts 3 and 14 are normative, the way for us to apply these passages today may be to pray for supernatural healing. While hospitals and medical ministries are wonderful ways to show God's love, it is supernatural healing that is described in these passages. Matthew's record of Jesus' words to the Twelve seems to agree with this, because the same verse that refers to healing the sick continues, "Raise the dead, cleanse the lepers, cast out demons" (Matt. 10:8). Casting out demons and raising the dead are certainly supernatural acts, and it seems that healing would have been understood in the same way.

6. The wording of Acts 14:21 (Paul and Barnabas "returned to Lystra and to Iconium and to Antioch") makes it clear

that the actions mentioned in Acts 14:22–23 ("strength-ening the souls of the disciples, encouraging them to continue in the faith" and having "appointed elders for them in every church") apply to the three cities men-tioned in verse 21. While Acts 14:21 starts out by saying that many disciples were made in Derbe, the text does not clearly say that a church was planted there. Lystra, Iconium and Antioch are the places that the sent-out ones "returned to," and these three cities provide the immediate setting for verses 22–23, in which the word *church* is mentioned. For this reason Lystra, Iconium and Antioch have been included in this book, while possible church plants in other cities mentioned in Acts, includ-ing Derbe, have not. A church may have been planted in Derbe, but the text does not specifically say so.

7. The Greek word translated "elders," *presbuteros* (πρεσβύτερος), is found eighteen times in Acts, more than in any other book of the New Testament. Sometimes it refers to old men (see 2:17) and sometimes it refers to the Jewish leaders (see 4:5, 8, 23; 6:12; 23:14; 24:1; 25:15). Ten times it refers to leaders in the churches (see 11:30; 14:23; 15:2, 4, 6, 22, 23; 16:4; 20:17; 21:18).

8. The Greek word translated "overseer" is *episkopos* (ἐπίσκοπος), which can also be translated "bishop."

9. The Greek word translated "shepherd" is *poimainō* (ποιμαίνω), the verb form of the word translated "pastor" in Ephesians 4:11.

10. It is true that some passages could be read as applying the word *elder* (interchangeable with *overseer* or *shepherd*) to a distinct group called *elders* (for example, 1 Tim. 5:17).

However, no passage requires a different understanding of the word *elder* than that which is the clear teaching of Acts 20.

11. While Apollos, in Corinth, provides an example of a church leader (see 1 Cor. 3:5–6) who was not an original member of the church (see Acts 18:24, 27), the New Testament norm seems to be to select leaders from among the church members.

12. The Greek word translated "church" in reference to Pisidian Antioch, Iconium and Lystra—*ekklēsia* (ἐκκλησία)—is the normal New Testament word for church.

13. See the discussion of Acts 2:41–47 in chapter 2 of this book, where characteristics of a healthy New Testament church are listed.

Chapter 6

1. The reason that Paul did not begin in the synagogue in Lystra may be that there was no synagogue there, but the text does not give a reason. It simply doesn't mention a synagogue.

2. The healing of this lame man, whom Paul noticed "had faith to be made well" (Acts 14:9), is different from that recounted in Acts 3, where the faith of the person about to be healed is not mentioned.

3. See the discussions of healing and signs and wonders in chapters 1, 2, 5 and 10 of this book.

4. The Greek word translated "language" is *dialektos* (διάλεκτος).

5. In forty-seven of the seventy-eight uses of the word *apostle* in the New Testament, the word seems to refer to the twelve apostles: Matthew 10:2; Mark 6:30; Luke 6:13; 9:10; 11:49; 17:5; 22:14; 24:10; Acts 1:2, 25, 26; 2:37, 42, 43; 4:33, 35, 36, 37; 5:2, 12, 18, 29, 40; 6:6; 8:1, 14, 18; 9:27; 11:1; 15:2, 4, 6, 22, 23; 16:4; First Corinthians 15:7, 9; Galatians 1:17, 19; 2:8; Ephesians 2:20; 3:5; First Peter 1:1; Second Peter 1:1; 3:2; Jude 17 and Revelation 21:14.

6. The twelve apostles are listed by name four times in the New Testament: Matthew 10:2–4, Mark 3:16–19, Luke 6:14–16 and Acts 1:13.

7. In eternity the twelve apostles are still recognized as a specific group. Revelation 21:14, speaking of the New Jerusalem in the new heaven and new earth, says that "the wall of the city had twelve foundation stones, and on them were the twelve names of the twelve apostles of the Lamb."

8. The command in Matthew 28:19 is to make disciples. *Go* is a participle that could be translated "as you go." The book of Acts pictures unnamed Christians, who had been dispersed by persecution, being scattered to Antioch, evangelizing, making disciples and planting a church (see Acts 11). Every Christian is commanded to evangelize and make disciples, according to the Great Commission.

9. Philip may be an example of one who was not a sent-out one, but who obeyed the Spirit's leading to go on a short trip (to meet the Ethiopian eunuch in the desert) before settling down to live for many years in one city (see Acts 8:25–40; 21:8).

10. With the words "the heaven and the earth and the sea and all that is in them" (Acts 14:15), Paul is quoting Psalm 146:6. His words are within one word of being an exact quote from the Septuagint (LXX), the Greek translation of the Old Testament used by Paul.

11. Acts 20:31 tells us that Paul stayed three years in Ephesus.

12. Paul habitually revisited churches that he had started, a pattern that we see in Acts 14:21, 15:41, 16:4–5 and 18:23.

13. The Greek word translated "elder" is *presbuteroi* (πρεσβύτερος), from which comes the English word *presbyter*.

14. The Greek word translated "oversight" is *episcopas* (ἐπίσκοπος), from which comes the English word *episcopal*, and which can be translated "bishop."

Chapter 7

1. Romans 12:8, describing the spiritual gift of encouragement, uses the same word, *paraklēsis* (παπάκλησις), that describes Barnabas in Acts 4:36.

2. There is no mention in Scripture of a church on Cyprus after Paul's first missionary journey. Barnabas persisted in visiting Cyprus in order to see a church planted on his home island.

3. See chapter 2 of this book, where the same kind of church multiplication into the surrounding region was noted about the Jerusalem church.

4. Acts 16:1 states, "Paul came also to Derbe and to Lystra," suggesting that Derbe and Lystra were not among the churches that Paul and Silas were strengthening at the close of Acts 15 (the churches in "Syria and Cilicia").

5. The "Macedonian call" is beautifully sung of in the 1800s hymn "Send the Light," which contains the phrase "We have heard the Macedonian call today, 'Send the light! Send the light!'" Although it refers historically to Paul's call to Macedonia, it is used metaphorically to speak of the believer's call to take the gospel to the lost.

6. Acts 16:10 is the first of the "we" passages in Acts, showing that Paul was traveling with a team. The other references to this are 16:10–17, 20:5–15, 21:1–18 and 27:1–28:16.

7. Paul's interaction with Lydia reminds us of the person-of-peace model, taught by Jesus, that was seen on Paul's first missionary journey. Paul entered the city of Philippi, spoke a spiritual word to those he came across (in faith that God had prepared some before he had arrived) and then centered his ministry in the home of those whom God had prepared.

8. We can see seven uses of the word *rejoice* in the book of Philippians: 1:18; 2:17, 18, 28; 3:1 and 4:4, 10.

9. The fact that the Philippians desired to follow Paul's teaching would be consistent with the believers in Acts 2:42: "They were continually devoting themselves to the apostles' teaching."

10. Acts 2:42 and Philippians 1:5 both use κοινωνία (*koinōnia*). The word is translated "fellowship" in Acts

2:42 and "participation" in Philippians 1:5. Both have to do with the believers' communing with each other, or sharing in common.

Chapter 8

1. Paul's custom may have been simply to go to a synagogue on the Sabbath, or it may have been to go to the synagogue and reason with people from the Scriptures (see Acts 17:2) as a part of his church-planting strategy, or custom.

2. In Acts 15:21 we are told that Moses, or Scripture, was "read in the synagogues every Sabbath." The same insight is found in Acts 13:15 and 27, where we see that Paul and Barnabas went to the synagogue, and the Law and the Prophets were read. It is significant that this is what the Holy Spirit chose to tell us about the synagogues: they are places where God's Word was read. An application of Paul's example for the church planter today might be to begin church planting with those who have already been reading Scripture. The broad seed sowing of exposing people to Scripture prepares hearts for church planting. See the discussion on abundant gospel sowing in chapter 4 of this book.

3. See the discussion of Lystra, where Paul did not follow his normal custom in presenting the gospel, in chapter 6 of this book.

4. We see examples of Paul commending new churches to the Lord and leaving them in Acts 20:32 and Romans 16:25–26.

5. We see a group of believers turning for the first time to the Greeks in Acts 11:20. See the discussion on contextualization in chapter 3 of this book.

6. In Acts 25 we see another instance of someone summarizing Paul's message: as Festus told King Agrippa about Paul, he stated that Paul's message was "about a dead man, Jesus, whom Paul asserted to be alive" (25:19). Those who heard Paul knew that he talked about Jesus and proclaimed that Jesus was alive from the dead.

7. While it is possible that churches were planted in more than nine cities in the book of Acts, in the nine cities that we examine in this book, the book of Acts specifically mentions a church being planted.

8. We know that it was "a short period of time" after he left Thessalonica that Paul sent workers to check on the believers because First Thessalonians 2:17 says he had "been taken away from [them] for a short while."

9. Acts 18:5 tells us that Silas and Timothy arrived in Corinth from Macedonia (the region in which Philippi and Thessalonica were located) with an offering. Philippians 4:15 makes it clear that the church at Philippi had sent an offering. We know also that Timothy had been sent to the Thessalonians (see 1 Thess. 3:2), so it appears that Silas had gone to Philippi, and the two returned to Paul together.

10. Others in Scripture followed God by night. Remember that Gideon, in the Old Testament, when commanded to build an altar to the Lord, "because he was too afraid of his father's household and the men of the city to do it by day, he did it by night" (Judg. 6:27).

11. See the discussion of the need for sent-out ones to be filled with the Holy Spirit in chapter 1 of this book.

12. *Us* in First Thessalonians 1:6—those whom the new believers "became imitators of"—refers to Paul, Silas and Timothy (see 1:1).

Chapter 9

1. See the discussion regarding Acts 11:26 and the year that Paul and Barnabas spent making disciples in Antioch in chapter 3 of this book.

2. Acts 18:4–7 describes Paul moving his ministry from the synagogue to the house of Titius Justus, but we are not told that he stayed anywhere else, suggesting that he continued to stay with Aquila and Priscilla.

3. See chapter 10 of this book for a discussion of the multiplication of disciples seen in Aquila and Priscilla's mentoring of Apollos.

4. See the discussion of the direction of the money flow in chapter 3 of this book. This topic is also discussed in chapter 7, regarding the church plant in Philippi.

5. Thessalonica is the city where Paul went after Philippi.

6. The Greek word for "shake out" is *ektinassō* (ἐκτινάσσω), and it is used only four times in the New Testament: in Matthew 10:14, Mark 6:11, Acts 13:51 and here in Acts 18:6. The two uses in the Gospels are in Jesus' teaching on the person-of-peace model. The other two uses, in Acts, show the model being applied. See the discussion on the person-of-peace model in chapter 4 of this book.

7. In telling the Jews that their blood would be on their own heads in Acts 18:6, Paul was referring to Ezekiel 33:8–9, where we read that God desires the salvation of the wicked (see 33:11) and sends a watchman to warn them; if the wicked repent at the warning of the watchman, they will be saved (see 33:14–15). If the watchman does not warn the wicked, however, the wicked will die in their sins, but their blood will be required of the watchman. If the watchman faithfully goes, and the wicked man does not heed the warning, "he will die in his iniquity, but [the watchman will] have delivered [his] life" (33:9). Paul was telling the Corinthian Jews that this last possibility was taking place.

8. First Corinthians 16:8 shows us that the book of First Corinthians was written from Ephesus, and Acts 19:10 seems to be where the writing of this letter fits into the flow of Acts. This would have been sometime during Paul's three-year stay in Ephesus—the first and primary stop of his third missionary journey.

9. Matthew 10:26, 28, 31 and Philippians 4:6, among other passages, tell us not to be afraid.

Chapter 10

1. Paul discipling Aquila and Priscilla, Aquila and Priscilla discipling Apollos, and Apollos discipling believers in Corinth is an example of disciples making disciples, or the multiplication of disciples.

2. As we have noted several times in the book of Acts, Paul never stayed longer in a place than three years, but for Paul leaving did not mean deserting. Paul continued to

train leaders and to disciple believers in a city for years after starting their church.

3. Further passages that talk about the Spirit's presence in a believer's life are Ephesians 1:13 and Titus 3:5.

4. The word *tongues* (*glōssais*, γλώσσαις) is found six times in the book of Acts (always in the plural, as here in Acts 19:6) and refers to three occasions. Four of the six mentions are in Acts 2, where the gift is clearly defined by the word *dialect*, referring to known languages. Tongues are mentioned for the fifth time in Acts 10:46 regarding Cornelius' household and for the sixth time here in Acts 19:6 regarding the disciples of John. The gift is not common in Acts. It would be best to understand all uses of the word *tongues* in Acts as referring to the same gift described in Acts 2. Acts 10:47, 11:15 and 11:17 use the words "just as" and "same" to stress the similarity and connection between the faith and experience of the Samaritans and that of those from Jewish background, apparently to demonstrate the unity of the church.

5. "Reasoning" is translated from the Greek *dialegomai* (διαλέγομαι), the root of the English word *dialogue*.

6. The words *church* (*ekklēsia*, ἐκκλησία) and *home* (*oikos*, οἶκος) are used together in the same verse four times in the New Testament (see Rom. 16:5; 1 Cor. 16:19; Col. 4:15; Philem. 1:2). No other venue is specified more often than a house as a place in which a church met.

7. See further discussion on signs in chapters 1, 2 and 5 of this book.

8. See the discussions on contextualization in chapter 3 of this book.

9. The occasion of Paul commanding an evil spirit to come out of a slave girl in Acts 16:18 and God's "performing extraordinary miracles by the hands of Paul" in Acts 19:11–12 are the only instances mentioning evil spirits during Paul's ministry in Acts. Two other mentions of unclean or evil spirits in Acts (for a total of four) are in Acts 5:16, when people afflicted with unclean spirits are being "healed" by Peter, and in Acts 8:7, when Philip comes to Samaria: "Many who had unclean spirits, they were coming out of them."

10. Later, in Acts 23:11, Jesus personally makes a promise to Paul similar to his declaration here in Acts 19:21 that he has to see Rome after going to Jerusalem.

11. The Greek word translated "to shepherd" is *poimainō* (ποιμαίνω); its verb form comes from the noun *poimēn* (ποιμήν), translated "pastors" in Ephesians 4:11.

12. See the discussion on the interchangeability of the words *overseer*, *elder* and *shepherd* in chapters 2, 5, 6 and 7 of this book.

13. See the discussion on working hard, day and night, in chapter 8 of this book.

PUBLICATIONS
Fort Washington, PA 19034

This book is published by CLC Publications, an outreach of CLC Ministries International. The purpose of CLC is to make evangelical Christian literature available to all nations so that people may come to faith and maturity in the Lord Jesus Christ. We hope this book has been life changing and has enriched your walk with God through the work of the Holy Spirit. If you would like to know more about CLC, we invite you to visit our website:

www.clcusa.org

To know more about the remarkable story of the founding of
CLC International we encourage you to read

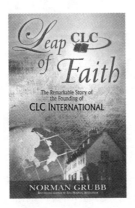

LEAP OF FAITH

Norman Grubb

Paperback
Size 5 1/4 x 8, Pages 248
ISBN: 978-0-87508-650-7
ISBN (*e-book*): 978-1-61958-055-8

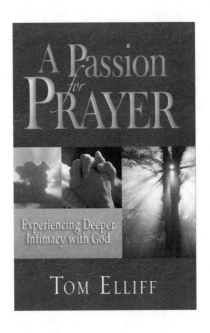

A PASSION FOR PRAYER

Tom Elliff

Of all the disciplines of the Christian life, prayer is perhaps the most neglected. Yet Jesus' brief earthly life was permeated with it. *A Passion for Prayer* seeks to help you develop—or deepen—your communion with God. Drawing on personal experience and God's Word, Pastor Tom Elliff shares principles for daily coming before the throne of grace.

Paperback
Size 5¹/₄ x 8, Pages 252
ISBN: 978-1-936143-03-0
ISBN (*e-book*): 978-1-936143-26-9